AF478506

PHILINE VON SELL
MADE IN GERMANY

PHILINE VON SELL
MADE IN GERMANY

HATJE CANTZ

VON DER WERTSCHÖPFUNG
HANS-JÖRG CLEMENT

»Ich verwende das Medium Fotografie, weil meine Arbeitsweise und die Arbeitsprozesse mit dem Potenzial des Augenblicks umgehen«, sagt Philine von Sell. Es sind diese kurzen, nur Sekundenbruchteile dauernden Momente, die von Sells Bilder und Geschichten entstehen lassen, welche sich mit der Vehemenz ihrer sinnlichen Kraft einbrennen und am Ende genau das Gegenteil des sich verflüchtigenden Augenblicks meinen: Sie lassen Außen- und Innensicht, An- und Einsicht ineinander aufgehen.

Die Arbeiten Philine von Sells verbinden daher die Dokumentation des Zufalls mit der Assoziation des Wesentlichen, das objektiv Vorgefundene mit der subjektiven Umgestaltung. Auf diesem Weg werden die Fotografien deutscher Fabriken und Manufakturen, ihrer Produkte und ihrer Fertigungsprozesse, ihrer alltäglichen Routine und den standardisierten Gesten zu Bildern mit ganz eigener Ästhetik und der Unverwechselbarkeit eines Fingerabdrucks. Dies spiegelt sich auch im formalen Vorgehen der Fotografin wider: Philine von Sell wählt das in den Blick genommene Motiv, macht ihre Aufnahmen ohne Stativ mit einer analogen Mittelformatkamera, akzeptiert ausschließlich das vorhandene Licht und verzichtet auf jegliche spätere Manipulation. Der Handabzug schließlich entspricht dem Respekt der Künstlerin demgegenüber, was sie mit der Kamera im schönsten Sinne des Wortes festhält. Die Finesse dieses Vorgehens und das zeitlose, fast klassische Vokabular finden ihre Entsprechung in der Wertigkeit der Produkte, denen sich Philine von Sell mit den hier vorgestellten Aufnahmen zuwendet.

Aus der beschriebenen Annäherung und Aneignung kommt diesem künstlerischen Projekt eine gesellschaftspolitische Relevanz zu, der sich die Konrad-Adenauer-Stiftung, die die Förderung von Kunst und Kultur als Satzungsaufgabe verankert hat, mit besonderem Engagement zuwendet: Philine von Sell dokumentiert und gestaltet, was sich in dem längst auf das pekuniäre Moment reduzierten Begriff Wertschöpfung verbirgt, nämlich den sich ergebenden, kostbaren Mehrwert jenseits aller Messbarkeit. Die Erkenntnis eines Moments der emotionalen Qualität, die sich über ein durchaus eben auch ästhetisch gespeistes kulturelles Gedächtnis erschließt und signalisiert: Hier geht es um individuelle – und am Ende vielleicht kollektive – Identität. Wer erinnert sich nicht, wie es sich anfühlt, einen Buntstift von Faber-Castell in der Hand zu halten, seine Kanten und den gelackten Knopf am Stiftende abzutasten? Solche Erinnerungen sind frei von aller konsumorientierten Oberflächlichkeit, sondern enthüllen – geradezu im Gegenteil – die Magie der perfekten Oberfläche, die sich als Teil des eigenen Innenlebens manifestiert hat.

Der Wirtschaftsstandort Deutschland besitzt viele Produktionsstätten, deren Erzeugnisse entscheidend zu unserer kulturellen (Aus-)Bildung beigetragen haben und Teil unserer Lebenswelt geworden sind. So selbstverständlich und beiläufig wie die Fotos von Philine von Sell – und ebenso nachhaltig. Das Durchblättern dieses Buches ist daher auch eine Entdeckungsreise, die sich durch die Mischung aus naturalistischem und verfremdendem Blick besonders spannend gestaltet und unmissverständlich deutlich macht, dass die meist menschenleeren Motive nichts anderes tun, als pausenlos auf den Menschen (und damit auf uns) zu verweisen. Hier geht es um das Nachspüren unserer Geschichte anhand von Traditionsunternehmen, was nichts mit einer mythisch aufgeladenen Übertreibung von Auftragsfotografie zu tun hat. Das unbestechliche künstlerische Auge von Philine von Sell ist selbstbewusst; und es ist unser Selbstbewusstsein, das sich in diesem Spiel aus Nähe und Distanz, aus Nüchternheit und Sympathie wiederfindet.

Die Konrad-Adenauer-Stiftung freut sich, ein Projekt zu begleiten, das gleichermaßen von künstlerischer Qualität wie von gesellschaftspolitischer Aussagekraft geprägt ist. Philine von Sell erinnert den Betrachter an die identitätsstiftende Schönheit von Alltagsprodukten und mahnt ohne didaktische Ambition die Wirtschaft, sich der prägenden ästhetischen Kraft ihrer Fertigung bewusst zu sein. Ansprechender kann die Verbindung von Sinnlichkeit und Verstand nicht sein.

ON CREATING VALUE
HANS-JÖRG CLEMENT

"I use the medium of photography because my work methods and processes involve the potential in the blink of an eye," says Philine von Sell. These fragmentary moments, lasting only split seconds, are created in von Sell's images and stories. They incandesce with the vehemence of her sensual power, till in the end they signify exactly the opposite of the self-dissipating blink of an eye. They give rise to intermixing exterior and interior vision, to views and to insights.

The works of Philine von Sell thus unite the documentation of coincidence with the association of the essential, the objective readymade with the subjective reconception. In this way, her photographs of German factories and manufacturing sites, their products and their assembly processes, their daily routines and standardized gestures, become images with an aesthetic all their own, as unique as a fingerprint. This is also reflected in the photographer's formal approach: von Sell selects a subject, shoots it without a tripod and with an analog medium-format camera, uses only available light, and makes no later manipulations of any kind. The handmade print shows solely the artist's respect for what she and her camera have, in the finest sense of the word, captured. The finesse of this approach and the timeless, almost classical vocabulary correspond to the high quality of the products that von Sell examines in the photographs presented here.

The proximity and appropriation described above give this artistic project a sociopolitical relevance, and for this reason the Konrad-Adenauer-Stiftung, founded in part with the aim of promoting art and culture, has engaged with it: Philine von Sell documents and shapes what lies hidden in the term *creating value*, which has long since been reduced to its pecuniary aspect: namely, the accumulating and precious added value that exists beyond all measurability. The recognition of a moment of emotional quality that also emerges from and is signaled by a very much aesthetically based cultural memory: these images are about individual—and ultimately perhaps also collective—identity. Who does not remember the feel of a Faber-Castell colored pencil in the hand, the texture of its contours and the painted knob at the top? These memories are free of any consumer-oriented superficiality. On the contrary: they reveal the magic of the perfect surface, manifested as a part of the individual's own inner life.

Many production sites in Germany make things that contribute decisively to our cultural formation and education, and that have become a part of our lives. These products have become as natural and casual as Philine von Sell's photos—and equally lasting. Paging through this book is thus a journey of discovery. It is an exciting journey in which the mixture of naturalistic and alienating vision makes unmistakably clear that the subject matter, for the most part devoid of human presence, does nothing other than refer ceaselessly to humans (and thereby to us as well). These works are about tracing our history through companies that have rich traditions; the works have nothing to do with a mythically fraught exaggeration of commissioned photography. The incorruptible artistic eye of Philine von Sell is self-confident; and we rediscover our own self-confidence in this play between nearness and distance, austerity and sympathy.

The Konrad-Adenauer-Stiftung is pleased to take part in a project that possesses artistic quality and sociopolitical expressiveness in equal measure. Philine von Sell reminds the viewer of the identity-endowing beauty of objects in daily life, just as she, free of didacticism, urges industry to be conscious of the aesthetic power of its products. The connection between sensuousness and understanding could not be more appealing.

KEIN FLÜSSIGES GOLD AUF UTOPIA …
ANNE MAIER

Das Gold liegt dunkel und dickflüssig auf der Palette, die Pinsel und Spachtel sind akkurat abgelegt. Arbeitspause. Man glaubt, eine Hand, wohl eine Frauenhand, zu sehen, wie sie seit Jahren rhythmisch unverdrossen und eben akkurat den Pinsel in die Farbe taucht. Sie trägt mit lockerem Schwung die dunkle, rotgelbe Farbe, das flüssige Gold, auf Teller und Tassen auf. Wir vermuten einen repetitiven Akt, er erscheint harmonisch und – entgegen der allseits benannten These vom sinnentleerten Tun des Arbeiters – als sinnvoll. Philine von Sell vermittelt etwas von der Würde der Arbeit, selbst wenn der Arbeiter auf dem Bild nicht zu sehen ist.

Mit Sozialromantik hat das nichts zu tun. Kein schöner Schein täuscht in den ausgewählten Motiven und dem Stil der Fotografien darüber hinweg, dass hier wie früher in einer Manufaktur – also von Hand und mit Verstand – ein Alltagsgegenstand gefertigt wird. Es befinden sich nur wenige Menschen in den riesengroßen Hallen, in denen Maschinen rattern, lärmen, Metall gegen Metall schlägt, Gummizüge quietschen und Loren, Gabelstapler oder sonstige Beförderungstechnik mit leichter Unwucht über die blank gebohnerten Estrichböden gefahren werden. Ab und an unterbricht ein Zischen den quälenden Lärm – als wollte der entweichende Dampf auf die ersten Stunden der Industrialisierung hinweisen, als mit Dampf betriebene Ungetüme in riesigen Fabrikfluchten eine Symphonie kakofonen Grauens aufführten.

Seither ist viel Zeit vergangen. Der Arbeiter an der Maschine ist heute vergleichsweise geschützt vor Lärm, Schadstoffen, zerstörerischen Arbeitsprozessen, ist selten überhaupt in den Fabrikgebäuden anzutreffen, zumindest im sogenannten alten Europa. Gilt doch der Mensch gemeinhin als berechenbarer Kostenfaktor, den zu minimieren zu einer ökonomisch wertvollen Tat geworden ist. Das stellte bereits John Ruskin fest, englischer Kunsthistoriker und Sozialphilosoph der beginnenden Industrialisierung. In seinen Maximen gegen die zunehmende Sinnentleerung menschlicher Tätigkeit in den englischen Fabriken entwickelte er eine Wirtschaftsethik, die den Menschen ins Zentrum der Aufmerksamkeit stellen und in der handwerklichen Arbeit den schöpferischen Anteil oder Wert erkennen sollte. Für Ruskin waren funktional effizient gestaltete Fabrikhallen bereits Synonyme für den Verfall der Qualität menschlicher Arbeit und ihrer Rezeption.

Die Dinge besitzen nur den Wert, den man ihnen beimisst, bemerkt der portugiesische Schriftsteller Fernando Pessoa in seinem *Buch der Unruhe*. In Zeiten des Paradigmenwechsels von der mechanischen Moderne zur digitalen Postmoderne ist dies ein geradezu exemplarisches Diktum, das die »gute Form« immer noch als etwas Greifbares, Handfestes versteht, zugleich die Formgebung im ephemeren Raum der digitalen, nicht mehr greifbaren Form nicht aus ihrer gestalterischen Verantwortung entlässt, Dinge für den Menschen zu schaffen.

Am Anfang des 21. Jahrhunderts haben globalisierte Entwicklungs- und Fertigungsprozesse die Objekte von ihren nationalen Markenzuordnungen oder gar Gütesiegeln »befreit«. Und sie haben ihnen damit zugleich jegliche Unschuld als Gegenstände der einstmals guten Form genommen, deren Wurzeln tief in einer Art »sozialer Plastik« verankert sind.

So gesehen müssen die Fertigungsbetriebe, die Philine von Sell in Deutschland besucht hat, wie Anachronismen erscheinen, Relikte einer Zeit, in der Arbeit von Hand zu Hand ging. Wohl in Anlehnung daran hat sie die hier porträtierten Produkte und – man ist versucht, sie so zu nennen – Manufakturen mit quasi analoger Sorgfalt »aus der Hand« fotografiert und in der Folge auch nicht digital bearbeitet.

Faber-Castell, Würth, Schleich, Rectus, Falke, Villeroy & Boch oder Dr. Oetker und alle weiteren Firmen stehen als Synonyme für eben dieses *Made in Germany*, für unternehmerische Sorgfalt und soziale Verantwortung. Ursprünglich waren es die Engländer, die mit dem »Merchandise Marks Act« von 1887 vor Waren und Produkten aus Deutschland warnten, also die heimische Produktion schützen wollten. Was als englisches Restriktionselement gedacht war, entpuppte sich als umgekehrte Erfolgsgeschichte. Die deutschen Produkte stellten sich in zunehmendem Maße als die qualitätvolleren heraus. Wobei zu berücksichtigen ist, dass in Deutschland viele industrielle sowie handwerkliche Verfahren vom damaligen Marktführer England übernommen, allerdings – nicht zuletzt in Zusammenarbeit mit den Kunstgewerbe-, später häufig Werkkunstschulen – präzisiert und verfeinert worden waren. So wurde aus dem Makel ein Prädikat. Der ursprünglich rein nationale Herkunftsnachweis geriet zum Gütesiegel in Herstellung und Produktion. »Ob es für Qualität bürgte, weil es deutsch war, oder ob es deutsch war, weil es für Qualität bürgte, lief schlicht auf das Gleiche hinaus.«[1]

Die hier abgebildeten Arbeitsprozesse sind dennoch immer Ausdruck industrieller Massenkultur, stehen für serielle Fertigung und Automatisierung. Und doch ist der sogenannte menschliche Faktor präsent. Die faber-castellschen Bleistiftminen werden nach wie vor von Hand (aus-)sortiert. Bei Eternit muss die Modularpaste von Hand auf die endlos aneinanderzufügenden Grundformen aufgetragen werden. Bausch Decor stellt Dekorpapiere her, die Holzmaserungen täuschend echt wiedergeben. Bevor auf riesigen Rollen das immer gleiche Muster in immer gleicher Intensität gedruckt werden kann, muss der Arbeiter die Farben anrühren, zusammenstellen und die Kombinationen finden und erkennen, die in Endlosschlaufe das immer gleiche Abbild einer Holzmaserung ergeben. Wie etwa beim Champagner der namhaften Hersteller, die immer gezwungen sind, eine Geschmacksidentität herzustellen.

Die Simulation ist perfekt, die endlose Wiederholung der Ereignisse und Vorgänge – die Mechanik – produziert das immer gleiche Objekt. Die Perfektion mutiert von der handwerklichen Exzellenz, das Singuläre schaffen zu wollen, zur indefiniten Beständigkeit. Die Ästhetik des Maschinenbaus orientiert sich alleine an der Effizienz ihres Ausstoßes.

Wolfgang Ruppert hält es für entscheidend, die Objektgeschichte offener und losgelöst von zu engen Begrifflichkeiten rund um das Artefakt zu sehen. In seinem »Plädoyer für den Begriff der industriellen Massenkultur« verweist er auf die veränderte Wahrnehmung seit den 1980er-Jahren und auf eine neue Aufgeschlossenheit der visuellen Rezeption der Objektwelt gegenüber.[2] Die Ästhetik des Seriellen hat seitdem jede Grenze geradezu spielerisch übersprungen. Die perfekte Realität, eine fehlerlose Welt, die die Maschinen in den Fertigungshallen durch immer gleiche Produktionsprozesse mit ihren sich beständig wiederholenden Geräuschen vorspielen, zeigt – in vielleicht bedrückender – Weise, dass seit Fritz Langs *Metropolis* aus dem Jahre 1927 ästhetisch kaum Zeit vergangen ist. Wohl hat der Beginn des Zeitalters technischer Reproduzierbarkeit unser Bewusstsein grundlegend verändert. Wir aber sind der Faszination des immer Gleichen erlegen und suchen beseelt nach dem Singulären, dem Fehler, dort, wo das Makellose das Maß aller Dinge ist.

Made in Germany ist Anachronismus und Zeitgeist gleichermaßen. Zwar werden vereinzelt Warften quasi in Handarbeit aufgeschüttet, doch die schöne neue Warenwelt des 21. Jahrhunderts liegt »Land unter«, umspült vom Weltmeer der Börsenkurse. Und deshalb sehnt man sich nach einem Orientierungspunkt, etwa der »guten Form« als substanziellem Wegweiser zum Nicht-Ort: Utopia.

1 Rainer Metzger, »Musterboden – Über die Logik des Labels ›Made in Germany‹ in der Kunst der Gegenwart«, in: *Made in Germany*, Ausst.-Kat. kestnergesellschaft, Hannover, Kunstverein Hannover, Sprengel Museum Hannover, Ostfildern 2007, S. 30–34, hier 33.
2 Wolfgang Ruppert, »Plädoyer für den Begriff der industriellen Massenkultur«, in: ders. (Hrsg.), *Lebensgeschichten. Zur deutschen Sozialgeschichte 1850–1950*, Opladen 1980, S. 153.

NO LIQUID GOLD ON UTOPIA...

ANNE MAIER

The palette is covered with dark and viscous gold, brushes and scrapers are accurately lined up. A hand, presumably a woman's hand, assiduously and regulary dips the brush into the paint, as it might have done for years before. She is applying the dark red color, the liquid gold, onto plates and cups with virtous strokes. We suspect a repetitive act, but it seems harmonious and—contrary to the theses of the devoidness of meaning of the worker's gestures—meaningful. Philine von Sell conveys the dignity of work, even if the worker cannot be seen in the image.

This has nothing to do with a romanticization of the worker. The choice of subjects and the style of the photographs do not prettify away the fact that this is manufacturing, where objects used in daily life are still produced with know-how, by hand. Only a small number of people are on the immense factory floors, where machines clatter and clang, metal strikes against metal, rubber belts squeak, and cars, forklift trucks, and other vehicles drive, slightly overladen, across the polished composition floor. Now and then a hissing interrupts the torturous din, as though the escaping steam wished to call to mind the first hours of the Industrial Revolution, when steam-powered monstrosities in gigantic factory spaces performed a symphony of cacophonous horror.

A lot of time has passed since then. The worker at the machine today enjoys much more protection from noise, toxic substances, and destructive work processes, and is seldom to be found in factory buildings at all, at least in so-called Old Europe. Insofar as people are regarded as a quantifiable cost factor, minimizing their presence has become economically valuable. This was already apparent to John Ruskin, the English art historian and social philosopher of early industrialization. In his maxims against the increasing erosion of meaning in English factory work, Ruskin developed an anthropocentric economic ethics that sought to identify the creative element or value in artisanal labor. For Ruskin, factories with functionally efficient designs were themselves synonyms for the decline in quality of human labor and its reception.

In his *Book of Disquiet,* the Portuguese writer Fernando Pessoa observes that things have only as much value as people attach to them. In the era of the paradigm shift from mechanical Modernism to the digital Postmodern, this is an almost exemplary dictum: that "good form" is still something solid and tangible. In other words, design in the ephemeral space of digital, no longer tangible form is not relieved of the responsibility of creating objects for people.

At the beginning of the twenty-first century, globalized processes of development and manufacturing have "liberated" objects from systems of national branding, indeed from seals of approval altogether. And in so doing these processes have also taken away any innocence the objects may have had as artifacts of erstwhile good form, deeply rooted in a sort of "social sculpture."

Viewed in this way, the assembly sites that Philine von Sell visited in Germany must seem like anachronisms, relics of a time in which work went from hand to hand. Accordingly, the artist has photographed the products portrayed here—there is the temptation to call them, in the literal sense, *manufactures*—"by hand," with an analog sort of care, and has not digitally manipulated them in any way.

Faber-Castell, Würth, Schleich, Rectus, Falke, Villeroy & Boch, or Dr. Oetker and all the other firms depicted are synonyms for just this *Made in Germany,* for entrepreneurial meticulousness and social responsibility. Originally it was the English who wished to protect domestic production; the Merchandise Marks Act of 1887 was intended to warn consumers against goods and products made in Germany. What was intended to restrict the flow of goods into England, however, turned out to succeed at doing the reverse. A growing number of German products proved to be of higher quality than the competition. It should be noted that many German industrial and artisanal techniques had been adopted from those used in England, the market leader of the time, though these techniques were then improved and refined, not least through the contributions of the schools of arts and crafts, and later, in many cases, the schools of applied art. Thus a stigma was transformed into a mark of distinction. What had been merely a statement of national origin became a seal of quality in manufacturing and production. "It was ultimately a matter of indifference wether it guaranteed quality because it was German or wether it was German because it guaranteed quality."[1]

The work processes photographed here are expressions of industrial mass culture, and stand for serial production and automatization. And yet the human factor is always present. Faber-Castell leads continue to be sorted by hand. The modular paste at Eternit must be spread by hand onto the basic forms, which fit together endlessly. Bausch Decor produces decor paper that reproduces wood grain with striking verisimilitude. Before the unvarying pattern can be printed with unvarying intensity on enormous rolls, a worker must mix and prepare the paints, finding and recognizing the combinations that will result in an endless loop of the unvarying likeness of a given wood grain. As with French champagne, a highly regarded name-brand producer is always compelled to produce a sameness in taste.

The simulation is perfect. The endless repetition of events and processes—the mechanics—produce the object that is always the same. Perfection mutates from the artisanal excellence of seeking to create something singular to creating indefinite constancy. The aesthetics of machine construction are oriented solely on the efficiency of its output.

Wolfgang Ruppert believes it is crucial to view the history of objects in a more open way, free of too-narrow concepts centered around the artifact. In his "Plea for the Concept of Industrial Mass Culture,"[2] he remarks on the changes in perception that have taken place since the 1980s, and on a new open-mindedness in the visual reception of the world of objects. In recent years, the aesthetics of the serial have almost playfully leaped across every boundary. The idea of a perfect reality, a world without flaws played at by the machines on factory floors, carrying out always uniform production processes with ceaselessly repeated sounds, shows, in a perhaps startling fashion, that almost no time has passed, aesthetically speaking, since Fritz Lang's *Metropolis* in 1927. Certainly our consciousness has changed fundamentally since the beginning of the age of technological reproducibility. Even so, we are haunted by the fascination of the constant. We quest soulfully after the singular, the error, exactly in that place where flawlessness is the measure of all things.

Made in Germany is anachronism and zeitgeist rolled into one. The occasional dwelling mound may be built up, as it were, by hand, yet the brave new world of goods in the twenty-first century remains a sort of floodplain, washed over by the ocean of world markets. And this is why we long for a point of reference, such as "good form," to serve as a substantial signpost to No-Place: Utopia.

1 Rainer Metzger, "Exemplary Ground—On the Logic of the Label 'Made in Germany' in Contemporary Art," in *Made in Germany*, exh. cat. kestnergesellschaft, Hannover, Kunstverein Hannover, Sprengel Museum Hannover (Ostfildern, 2007), p. 38.
2 Wolfgang Ruppert, "Plädoyer für den Begriff der industriellen Massenkultur," in ibidem, ed., *Lebensgeschichten. Zur deutschen Sozialgeschichte 1850–1950* (Opladen, 1980), p. 153.

GEDANKEN ZU DEN FOTOGRAFIEN PHILINE VON SELLS

PETER FUNKEN

Philine von Sells Fotoprojekt *Made in Germany* zeigt Momente, Situationen und Impressionen aus der Welt der Arbeit in der deutschen Industrie. Für ihr Projekt fragte die Künstlerin bei zehn renommierten Unternehmen an und besuchte Produktionsstätten im ganzen Land. Ihre Fotografien zeigen Herstellungsverfahren und Produktion aus der Perspektive unvoreingenommen Interesses und damit unter einem Blickwinkel, der das Typische und Besondere im scheinbar Normalen und Routinierten erkennt.

So entstanden in den Jahren 2006 bis 2008 Werke, die die maschinelle und manuelle Arbeit, das Material und seine Verwandlung vom Rohstoff bis zum Endprodukt in den Unternehmen zeigen – all dies als Resultat einer künstlerisch-fotografischen Wahrnehmung und Tätigkeit, die sich ihrem Untersuchungsgegenstand aufgeschlossen und behutsam annähert. Die Fotografien in diesem Band wurden mit einer Pentax-Kamera im Mittelformat 4,5 x 6 Zentimeter hergestellt. Das Projekt ist noch nicht abgeschlossen und soll weitergeführt werden.

Made in Germany besichtigt die moderne Realität der Produktion vor allem unter dokumentarischen Gesichtspunkten. Beim Betrachten der entstandenen Fotoserie gewinnt man den Eindruck, dass sich für die Fotografin in der Arbeitwelt immer wieder neue, völlig überraschende Gesichtspunkte ergeben haben, dass sich ihr eine Welt aufgetan hat, die sie aufgrund ihrer Komplexität, Präzision und Effizienz erstaunte. In ihren Arbeiten werden äußerst unterschiedliche Produktionswirklichkeiten dargestellt, so wie sie die Fotografin erlebte – mit dem ihr eigenen frischen und unverbrauchten Blick und in Form eines Sehens, das dem Arbeits- und Herstellungsprozess großen Respekt zollt.

Die Aufnahmen zeigen das jeweils Spezifische der Industrieunternehmen, denn bei der Fertigung so verschiedener Produkte wie beispielsweise Keramik, Schrauben oder Lebensmittel wirken das Material und auch seine Bearbeitung sehr deutlich auf die direkte Umgebung ein. So sind die Fertigungsstätten bei Dr. Oetker, Bausch Decor, Falke, Rectus, Würth, Eternit, bei der Banknotendruckerei Giesecke & Devrient und weiteren führenden deutschen Unternehmen sowohl geprägt von den zu verarbeitenden Grundsubstanzen als auch durch technische und handwerkliche Erfordernisse bei der Herstellung, Sortierung und Lagerung dieser Qualitätsprodukte. Jedes Unternehmen besitzt somit etwas Außergewöhnliches und Unverwechselbares. Dies zeigt sich charakteristisch im Fertigungsprozess, an den Werkbänken und Arbeitsplätzen ebenso wie in Ordnungs- und Unordnungssystemen und selbstredend auch in der Architektur der Produktionsstätten.

So unterschiedlich wie die Produkte und ihre Herstellung, so verschieden sind auch die Fotografien, die Philine von Sell für das Projekt *Made in Germany* herstellte, denn bei jedem der Unternehmen ließ sie sich aufs Neue auf eine unbekannte Situation ein und entwickelte für jede Produktionssituation eine adäquate Form der Besichtigung: Da ist beispielsweise das mit *Zahlen* betitelte Foto, das in einer Produktionshalle bei Villeroy & Boch entstand (Abb. S. 87). Hier werden keramische Produkte gezeigt, die in Paletten zur Weiterverarbeitung aufgestellt wurden. Auf diesem Foto ist die Zwischenlagerung vor allem als Ordnungsvorgang dargestellt: Frontal erfasst und in einem ausgewogenen Verhältnis zwischen Horizontalen und Vertikalen betont die Komposition das Serielle der Fertigung. Anders als bei der Farbstiftherstellung stehen die Gegenstände hier in Reih und Glied und sind durch exakte Abstände voneinander getrennt. Zudem sind die Chargen wegen des Produktionsablaufes mit Ordnungszahlen versehen, deren Systematik sich nur den »Eingeweihten« erschließt.

Ein kurzer Rückblick: Die Welt der Industrie und der Produktion aufzunehmen und vorzustellen, war seit Mitte der 1920er-Jahre immer wieder das Anliegen moderner Fotografen. Mit der Industriefotografie, der Industriereportage und der sogenannten Sach- und Materialfotografie fanden im Medium absolut neue Einblicke in die moderne Welt statt, in ihre technische Realität und ihre produktive Gegenständlichkeit. Äußerst berühmt wurde Albert Renger-Patzsch (1897–1966) mit seinen Fotografien und Fotobüchern, etwa dem Bildband *Die Welt ist schön* (1928), in dem er Strukturähnlichkeiten zwischen Natur und moderner Technik, Parallelen zwischen biologisch gewachsener und technisch konstruierter Wirklichkeit vorstellte. Renger-Patzsch betrachtete das Fotografieren keineswegs als Kunst, vielmehr sprach er in seinen theoretischen Schriften vom »photographischen Handwerk« und förderte die Einheit von Technik und Mitteln. Seine »sachlichen Photographien«, die als Resultat seiner Vorstellungen von den Aufgaben des Mediums entstanden, waren innerhalb der sich entwickelnden, sogenannten »künstlerischen Photographie« revolutionär.[1]

Ein Teil der Fotografien Philine von Sells scheint im Grenzbereich zwischen realem und surrealem Bild angesiedelt, vor allem solche Werke, die Vorstellungen jenseits des eigentlichen Produkts zu evozieren wissen. Zu dieser Gruppe von Motiven gehört ein aus der Aufsicht geschossenes Foto, das eine rote Tischfläche zeigt, auf der eine Metallschaufel liegt, in der noch Spuren grünen Pigments zu erkennen sind (Abb. S. 42). Mit diesem Werkzeug werden bei Faber-Castell Farbstoffe aus den

Behältnissen genommen. Der Gegenstand erscheint vor dem tiefroten Untergrund der Tischplatte als absolut reduzierte Form – wie ein Idol aus einer anderen Kultur oder eine moderne Skulptur.

Dass die Künstlerin solche Beobachtungen in der Produktion machte, zeugt von ihrer genauen Wahrnehmung der Wirklichkeit, denn sie entdeckt immer wieder Außergewöhnliches im Alltäglichen. Mit diesem fotografischen Ansatz lässt sich dann letztlich begründen, warum Philine von Sell nur in Ausnahmefällen Menschen bei der Arbeit zeigt, denn ihr geht es vor allem um die großen Zusammenhänge, um die Atmosphäre in den Betrieben. Bei solchen Bildern aus der Produktion treten Menschen nur in Ausnahmefällen in Erscheinung, doch trifft man in den Fotos immer wieder auf Spuren ihrer Existenz und ihrer Tätigkeit.

Philine von Sell zeigt, welche Formen und Gegenstände die Arbeiter herstellen und welche Orte sie mit ihrem Handwerk bestimmen – jedoch nur ausnahmsweise, wie von Menschenhand gearbeitet wird. Philine von Sell geht es dementsprechend nicht um Porträts, um Gesichter, Gesten oder Haltungen bei der Arbeit, sondern um die Darstellung von Arbeitszusammenhängen und um die technisch-organisatorischen Bedingungen in den Fabriken. Der Mensch – und damit entspricht ihre Fotografie der heutigen Arbeitswirklichkeit – ist zwar nach wie vor unersetzlich, denn sein Geschick, seine Intelligenz und seine feinmotorischen Fähigkeiten lassen sich längst noch nicht überall durch Maschinen ersetzen, doch wird der in der Produktion arbeitende Mensch heute im Verhältnis zu früheren Epochen in immer geringerer Zahl benötigt. Der Mensch, nach wie vor für die heutige Produktion eminent wichtig, ist eigentlich zu einer ephemeren Größe geworden – so auch im Fotoprojekt *Made in Germany*. Gleichwohl erscheinen Werktätige in einigen wenigen Fotografien; dann stehen die Arbeiter im Zentrum des Geschehens, weil die Fotografin ihre Tätigkeit im Zusammenspiel mit den Maschinen und den Objekten vorstellt. Zwar sind die Töpferscheiben bei Villeroy & Boch unbesetzt, man erkennt aber deutlich, dass an diesen Arbeitsplätzen handwerklich-kreativ gearbeitet wird.

Es ist zudem die klare und ausgewogene Tektonik der Fotografien Philine von Sells, die eine deutliche Sprache spricht und die Qualität ihrer Bilder bestimmt. In den Kompositionen ihrer Fotografien werden immer wieder Ordnungkonzepte und Arbeitssysteme sichtbar, die unabdingbar sind, wenn tagtäglich von neuem ein hoher Produktionsstandard erreicht werden soll, der das Gütesiegel *Made in Germany* verdient. »Es ist eine

Sache eine Hochleistung zu erbringen, aber dies immer wieder zu schaffen, also permanent Güte und Qualität zu garantieren, das ist etwas Außergewöhnliches – das verbinde ich mit dem Begriff Made in Germany«, sagt Philine von Sell, und fährt fort: »Alles hat eine Seele – und nicht nur die Menschen, auch die Dinge haben eine Ehre.« Diese Formulierung mag tatsächlich für *Made in Germany* grundlegend gewesen sein, doch wirkt in der globalisierten Industrie der Gegenwart vor allem der moderne Designgedanke und somit die Idee von der Weiterentwicklung und vor allem der Verbesserung von Produktion und Produkten. Beim Design geht es um Waren und ihre Preise. Dies setzt Funktionalität und Funktionieren voraus und eben darin liegt eine große Stärke der deutschen Industrieprodukte. Der künstlerische Blick überformt diese Tatsache mit einer subjektiven Betrachtung – und dies scheint vonnöten, um überhaupt einen Blick für das zeitgenössische Industrielle zu entwickeln, denn eigentlich kennen wir als Konsumenten vor allem die Waren, kaum aber die Situation ihrer Produktion.

Aber es ist auch so, dass die Grenzen zwischen Design und Kunst im Schmelzen begriffen sind, dass es Überschneidungen zwischen beiden Bereichen gibt, ohne damit gleich zu behaupten, wir lebten in einer künstlerisch gestalteten Wirklichkeit. Es mag aber sein, dass dies ein noch verborgenes, bislang nicht vollständig begriffenes und nur halb bewusstes Anliegen der Moderne und ihrer Ausläufer ist. Erst die Zukunft wird uns darüber Aufschluss geben können. Doch wäre es dann eine der letzten, wenn auch eine der größten Utopien, die uns aus der Moderne des 20. Jahrhunderts bis in die Gegenwart leuchtet. Dies vom Ansatz her erkannt und in Fotografie umgesetzt zu haben, ist das Verdienst Philine von Sells, die ihre künstlerisch-persönliche Sichtweise zum Ausgangspunkt der großen Recherche *Made in Germany* gemacht hat.

1 Ingeborg Güssow, »Die neusachliche Photographie«, in: *Kunst und Technik in den 20er Jahren. Neue Sachlichkeit und gegenständlicher Konstruktivismus*, Ausst.-Kat. Städtische Galerie im Lenbachhaus, München 1980, S. 97 f.

THOUGHTS ON THE PHOTOGRAPHS OF PHILINE VON SELL

PETER FUNKEN

Philine von Sell's photography project *Made in Germany* depicts moments, situations, and impressions of the world of labor in German industry. The artist sought out ten renowned German firms and visited their production sites, all over the country. Her photographs show manufacturing and production processes from a dispassionate perspective that recognizes the essential and the exceptional in the seemingly normal and routinized.

The project includes works created between 2006 and 2008 that depict mechanized and manual labor, as well as the on-site transformation of raw material into final product. All of this results from the artist-photographer's perception and activity, unfolding and carefully examining an object of inquiry. The photographs in this volume are taken with a 4.5 x 6 cm medium-format Pentax camera. The project is not finished, and Philine von Sell has plans to continue with it.

Made in Germany emphasizes the documentary aspects of viewing the modern reality of production. This series gives an observer the impression that the photographer discovered in the world of labor a succession of new and utterly surprising perspectives. It seems that a world opened up to the artist, one that amazed her with its complexity, precision, and efficiency. The photographer's works present the very different production realities that she experienced—to which she devoted her own fresh gaze, in the form of a vision that shows great respect for the processes of labor and manufacturing.

The photographs show the specific characteristics of each industrial operation. In the manufacture of goods as various as ceramics, screws, and food products, it is clear that both raw materials and their processing will exert an influence over the immediate environment. The production sites of Dr. Oetker, Bausch Decor, Falke, Rectus, Würth, Eternit, the banknote printers Giesecke & Devrient, and other leading German companies are characterized both by the materials they use and by the technological and artisanal demands of the production, sorting, and storage of their high-quality goods. In this way, each firm possesses something exceptional, something unmistakably its own. Each manufacturing process, work bench, and workplace has something distinctive, as does each organizational system (or lack thereof), and, needless to say, each production site's architecture.

The photographs that Philine von Sell produced for *Made in Germany* are as various as the products and their manufacturing. This is because she immersed herself in a new situation at each new firm, developing an appropriate form of viewing for each new situation: For example, the photograph entitled *Zahlen* (Numbers), made in a Villeroy & Boch factory (ill. p. 87), shows ceramic products arranged in pallets awaiting finishing. This photograph presents interim storage as an organizational process: the composition is a frontal view, with a balance between the horizontal and the vertical that emphasizes the serial aspect of manufacturing. In contrast to the production of colored pencils, for example, the objects here stand in rank and file, set apart from one another by precise, repeating distances. In addition, the production process dictates that the batches be labeled with reference numbers comprehensible only to the "initiated."

A brief look back: in the years since the mid-1920s, modern photography has often been concerned with photographing and conceptualizing the world of industry and production. Industrial photography, industrial reportage, and so-called objective and material photography allowed for dramatic new insights into the modern world, into its technological reality and its productive specificity. Albert Renger-Patzsch (1897–1966) gained prominence through his photography and photo books, such as the volume *Die Welt ist schön* (The World Is Beautiful, 1928), in which he displayed structural similarities between nature and modern technology and parallels between biologically evolved and technologically constructed reality. Renger-Patzsch did not regard photography as an art. Instead, he spoke in his theoretical writings of "photographic handicraft" and argued for the unity of method and means. His "objective photographs," drawn from his ideas on the tasks of the medium, were revolutionary within the emerging field of "artistic photography."[1]

Certain of Philine von Sell's images seem to occupy a borderland between the real and the surreal, in particular those works that evoke conceptions that go beyond the actual product. Among this group is a photo shot from above showing the surface of a red table, atop which is a metal bucket bearing traces of green pigment (ill. p. 42). The bucket is a tool used at Faber-Castell to scoop pigment out of bins. Against the deep red background of the tabletop, the subject appears as a form that has been utterly reduced—like an idol from another culture, or a modern sculpture.

Such observations bear witness to the artist's precise perception of reality, which she uses to discover exceptional things in the everyday. This approach to photography is ultimately also the reason why Philine von Sell only infrequently shows people at work: her main interest lies in the broader context, the atmosphere of the factories. Though people rarely enter into such images of production, the photos often contain traces of their existence and activities.

Philine von Sell shows the forms and objects that workers produce, and the sites that they affect. Yet she does so only as an exception, much as labor by hand is the exception rather than the rule. Von Sell is not interested in portraits, faces, gestures, or attitudes at work, but rather in the depiction of contexts of work, and in the technological and organizational conditions of factories. Her photography corresponds to the reality of work today. Humans are still irreplaceable, since it is not yet close to possible to replace human ability, intelligence, and fine motor skills with machines; yet the number of humans required for a given quantity of production is lower now than at any prior epoch in history. Though humans are still eminently important for production, they have in fact become an ephemeral quantity—which is reflected in *Made in Germany*. On the other hand, when workers do appear, in a small number of photographs, they are at the center of the action, with the photographer presenting the interplay of their activities with machines and objects. The potter's wheels at Villeroy & Boch stand empty, yet it is clear that creative artisanal work is done at these workstations.

What is more, the clear and balanced tectonics of von Sell's photographs speak in a clear language, and define the quality of her images. Her compositions bring into view organizational concepts and work systems that are indispensable for the achievement of the high daily standard of production worthy of the seal "Made in Germany." "It is not only a matter of high performance, but of high performance sustained—of guaranteeing permanently high performance and quality. That is something exceptional—and that is what I associate with the term 'Made in Germany,'" says von Sell. She goes on: "Everything has a soul— not only people, but things, too, have their honor." Indeed, this formulation may have been fundamental to *Made in Germany*, but in today's globalized industry modern design concepts that emphasize the ongoing development and improvement of production and of products are most important. Design involves goods and their prices. Functionality and functioning are key, and it is precisely these aspects that are two of the great strengths of German industrial goods. The artistic gaze transforms this fact through subjective observation—which seems necessary to get a look into contemporary industrial activities at all; after all, as consumers we are familiar with goods, but not very familiar with how they are produced.

But it is also true that the boundaries between design and art are now being erased, such that areas of overlap exist between the two realms. This does not necessarily mean that our entire reality has been artistically shaped. There may be, however, a still-hidden issue here for Modernism and its successors, an issue not yet fully grasped, still half-conscious. Only time will tell us more. It may be that one of the last, if one of the greatest, utopias is illuminating our path out of the Modernism of the twentieth century into the present. To have recognized this methodologically, and to have realized it through photography, is the achievement of Philine von Sell, who has made her personal way of seeing the point of departure for the major inquiry that is *Made in Germany*.

1 Ingeborg Güssow, "Die neusachliche Photographie," in *Kunst und Technik in den 20er Jahren. Neue Sachlichkeit und gegenständlicher Konstruktivismus*, exh. cat. Städtische Galerie im Lenbachhaus (Munich, 1980), pp. 97–98.

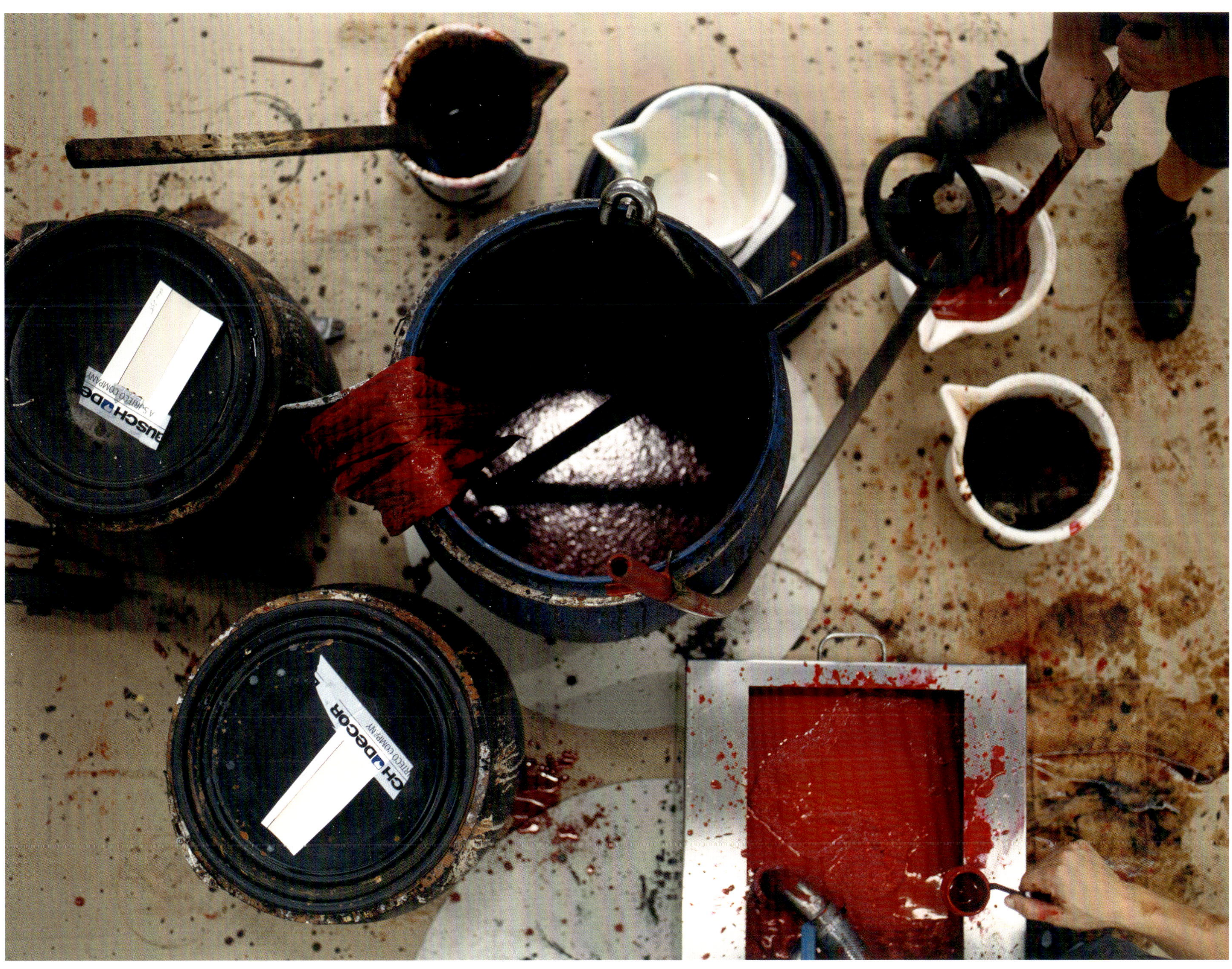

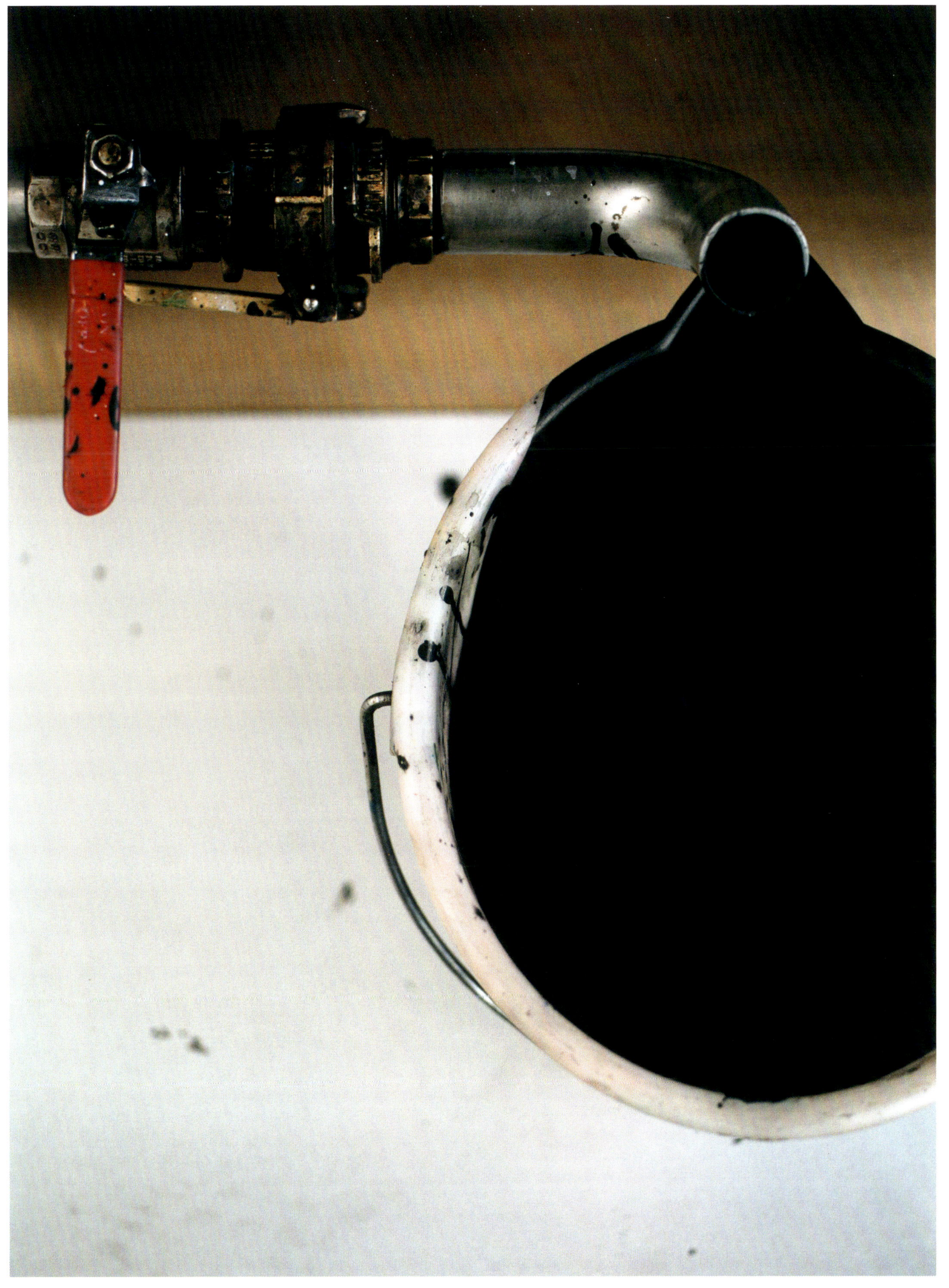

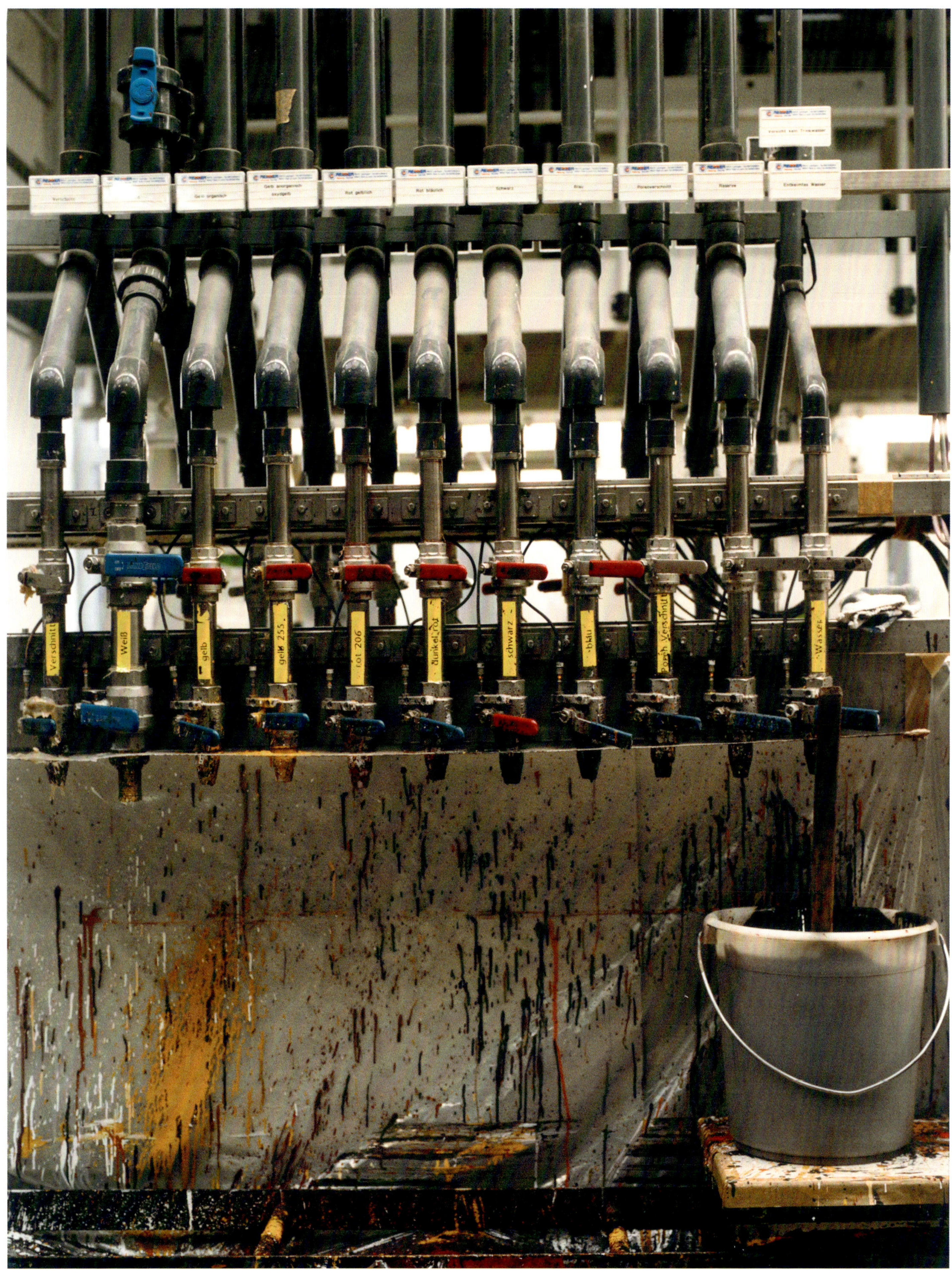

Versuch vom Trinkwasser
Verschnitt
Gelb organisch
Gelb anorganisch oxydgelb
Rot gelblich
Rot bläulich
Schwarz
Blau
Farbverschnitt
Reserve
Entkalktes Wasser
Verschnitt
Weiß
gelb
gelb 255.
rot 206
dunkel/rot
schwarz
blau
Farb. Verschnitt
Wasser

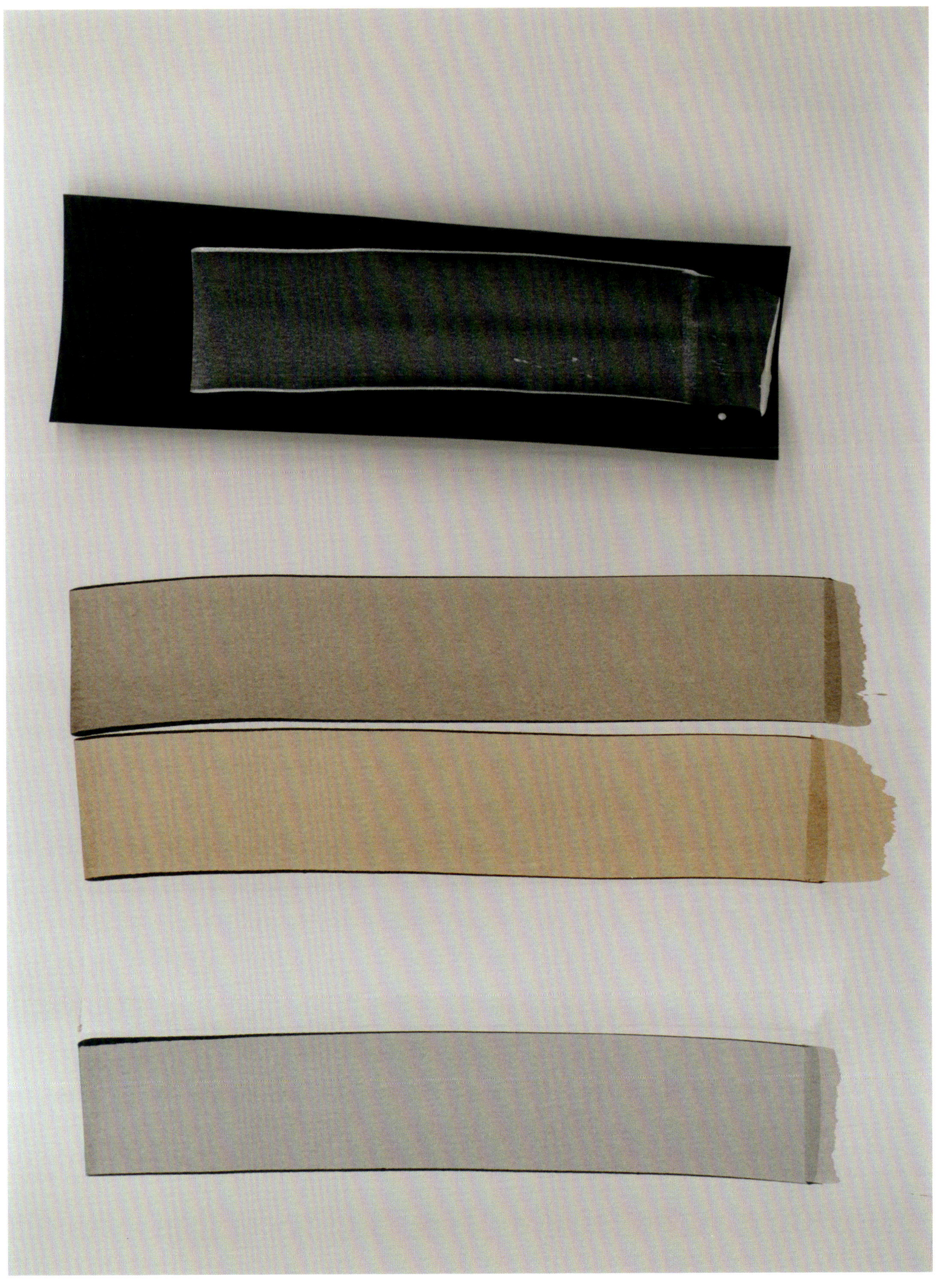

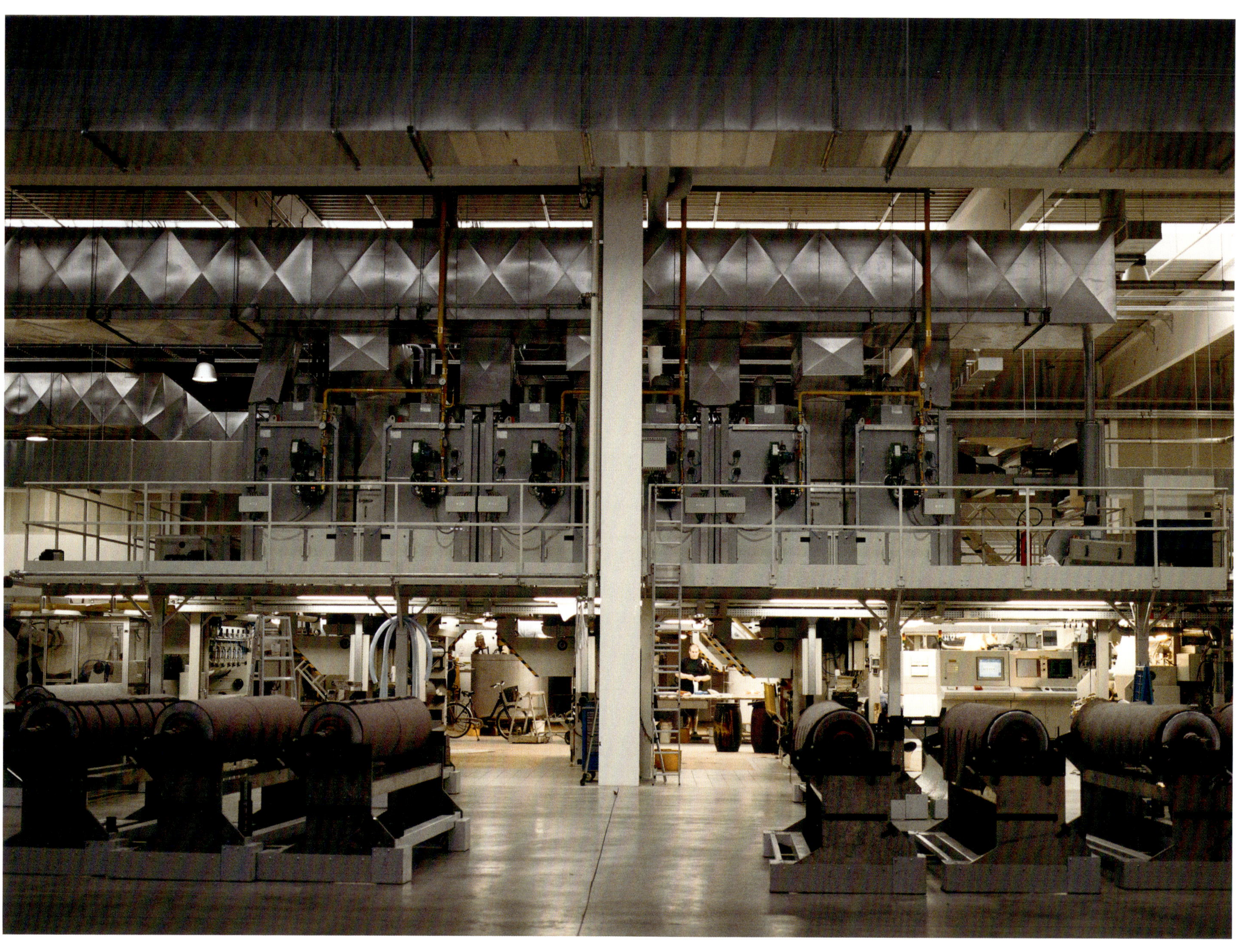

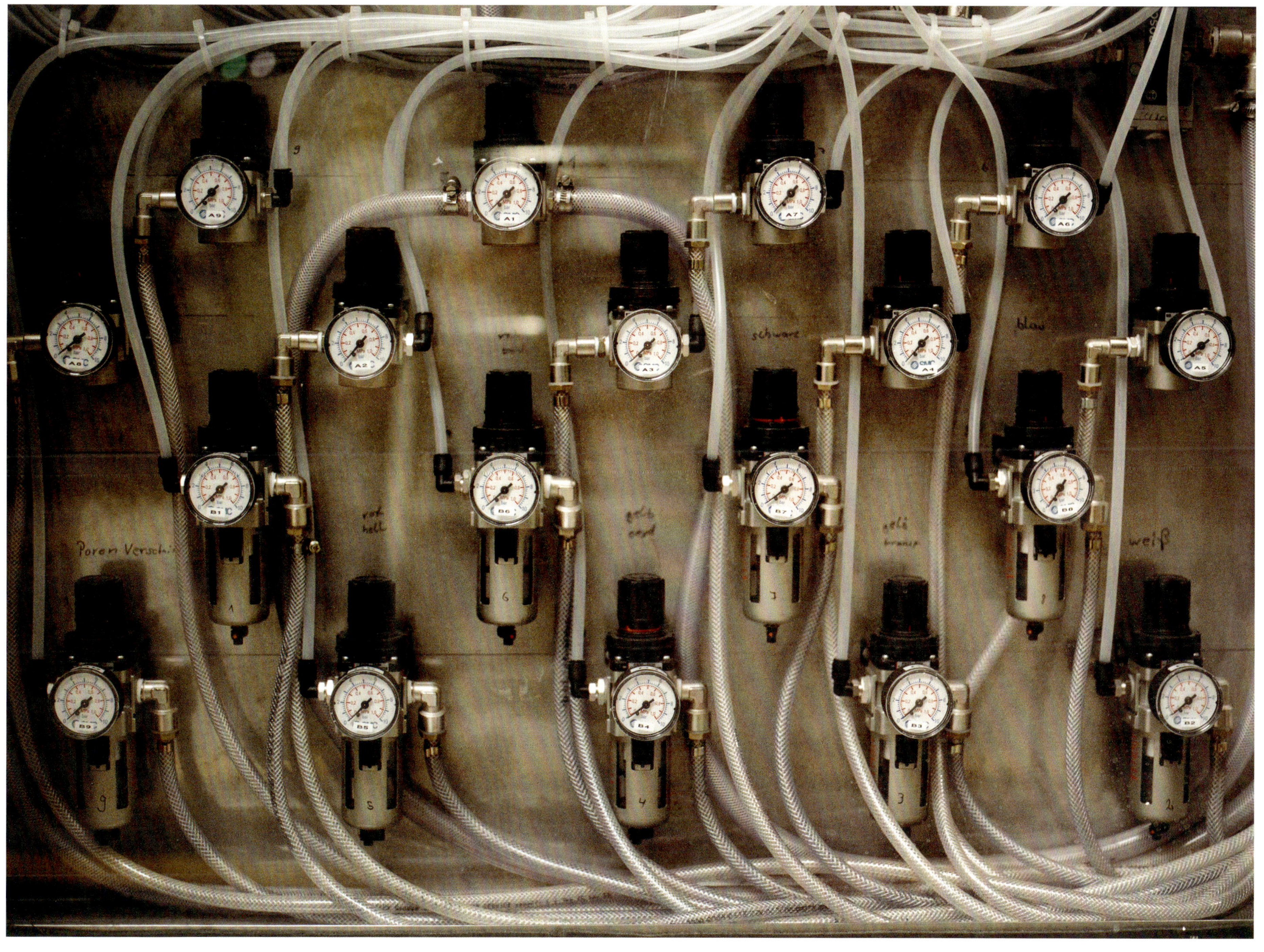

schwarz
blau
Poren Verschl
rot hell
gelb oral
gelb braun
weiß

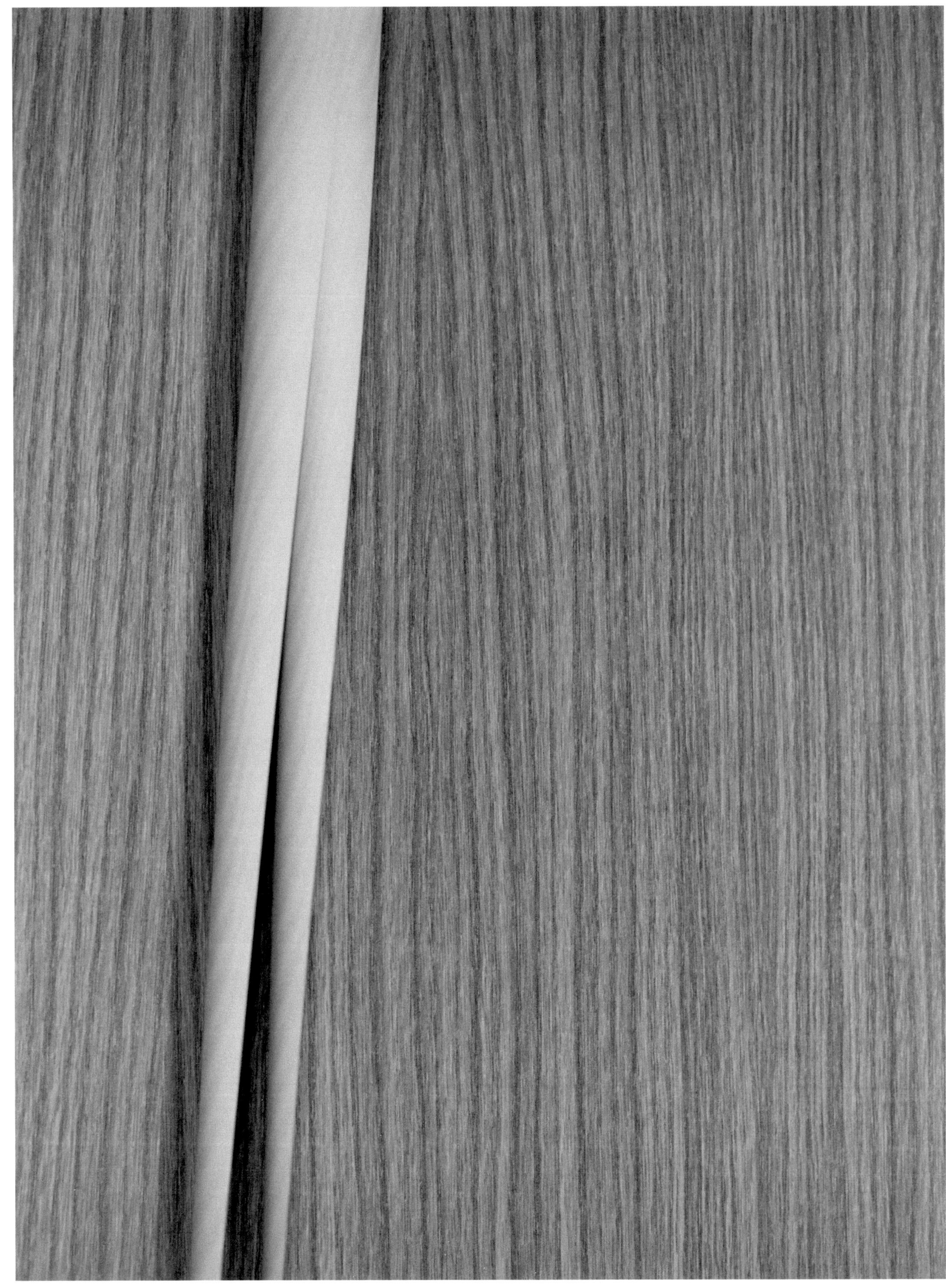

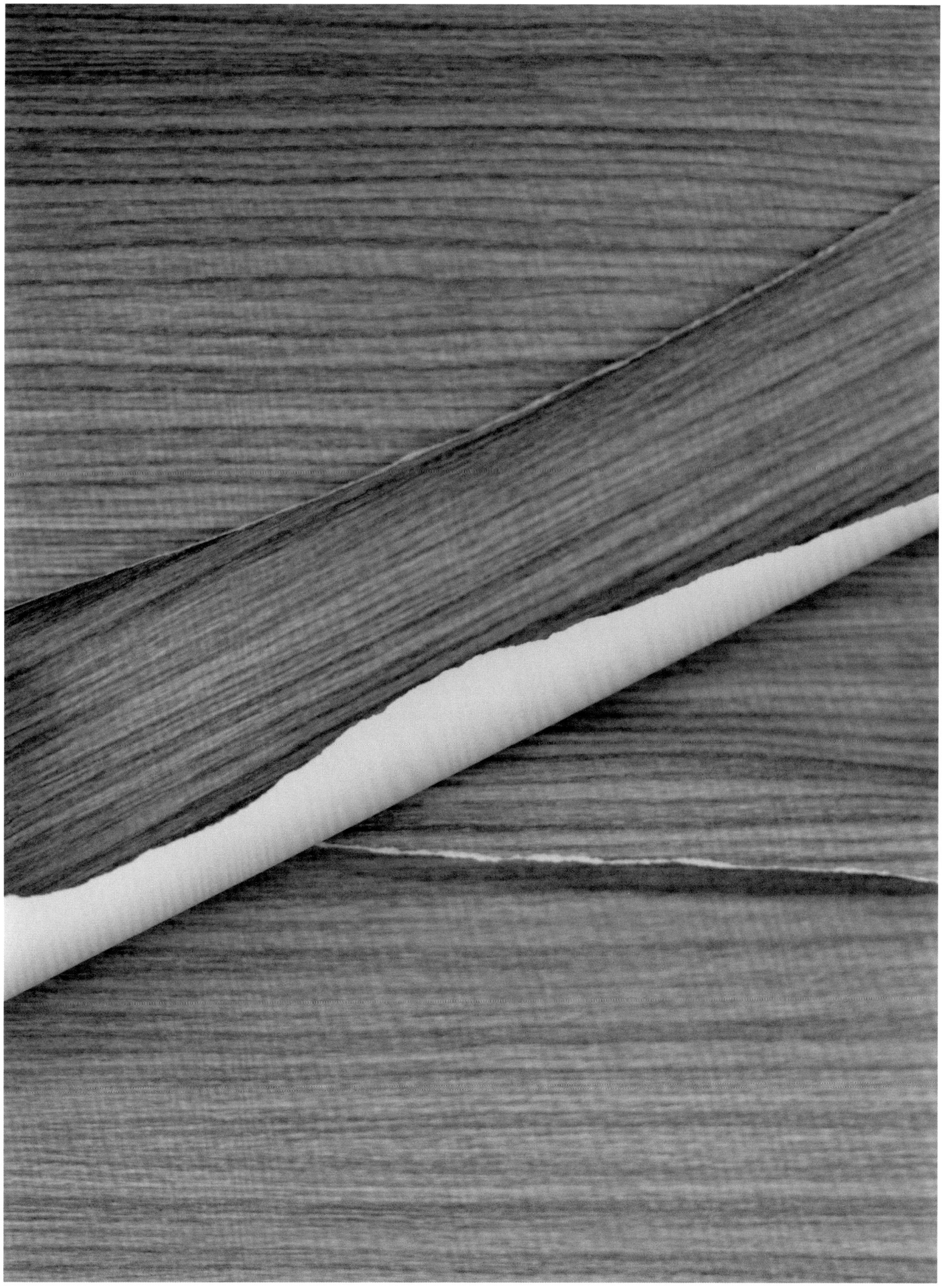

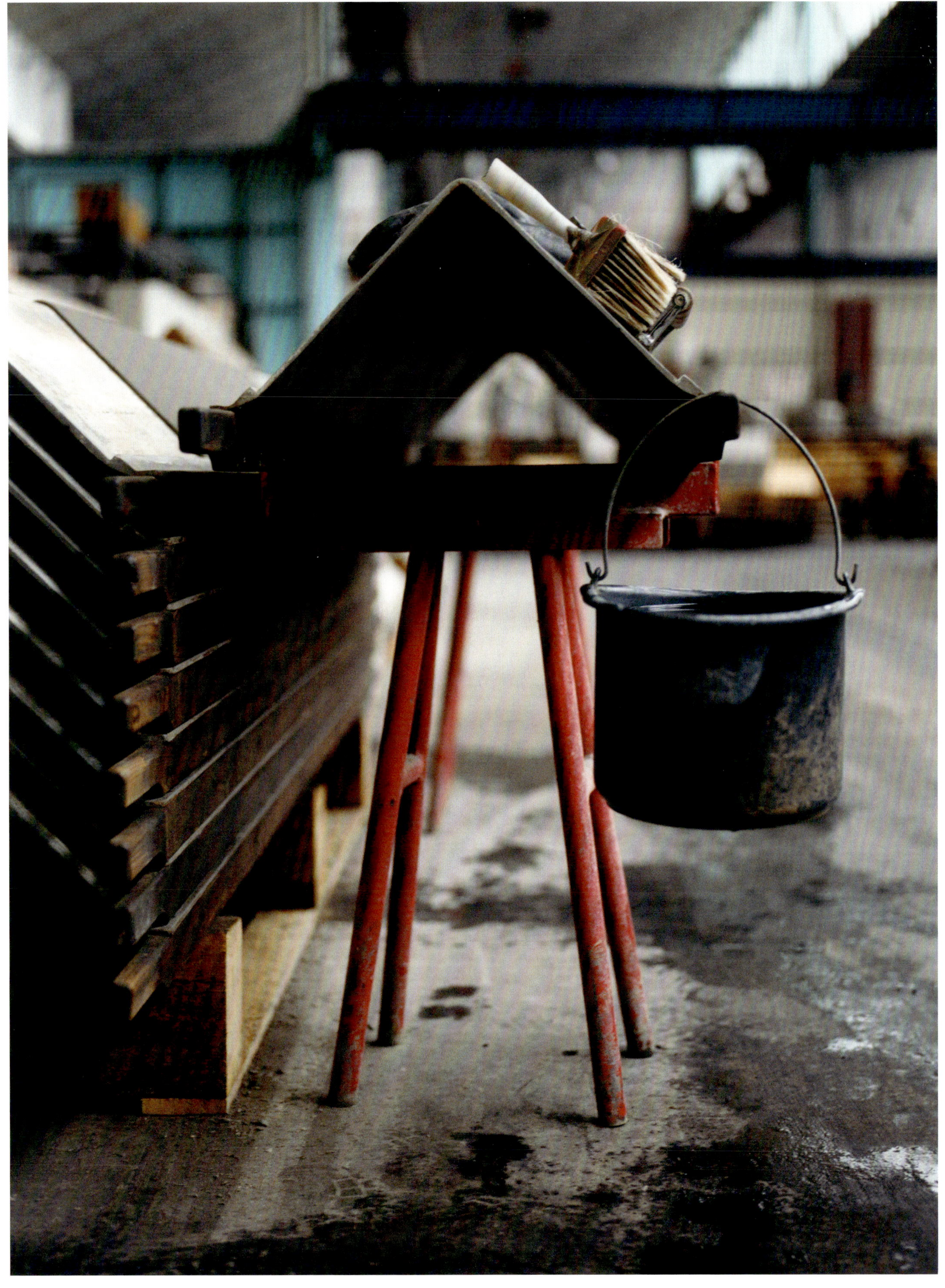

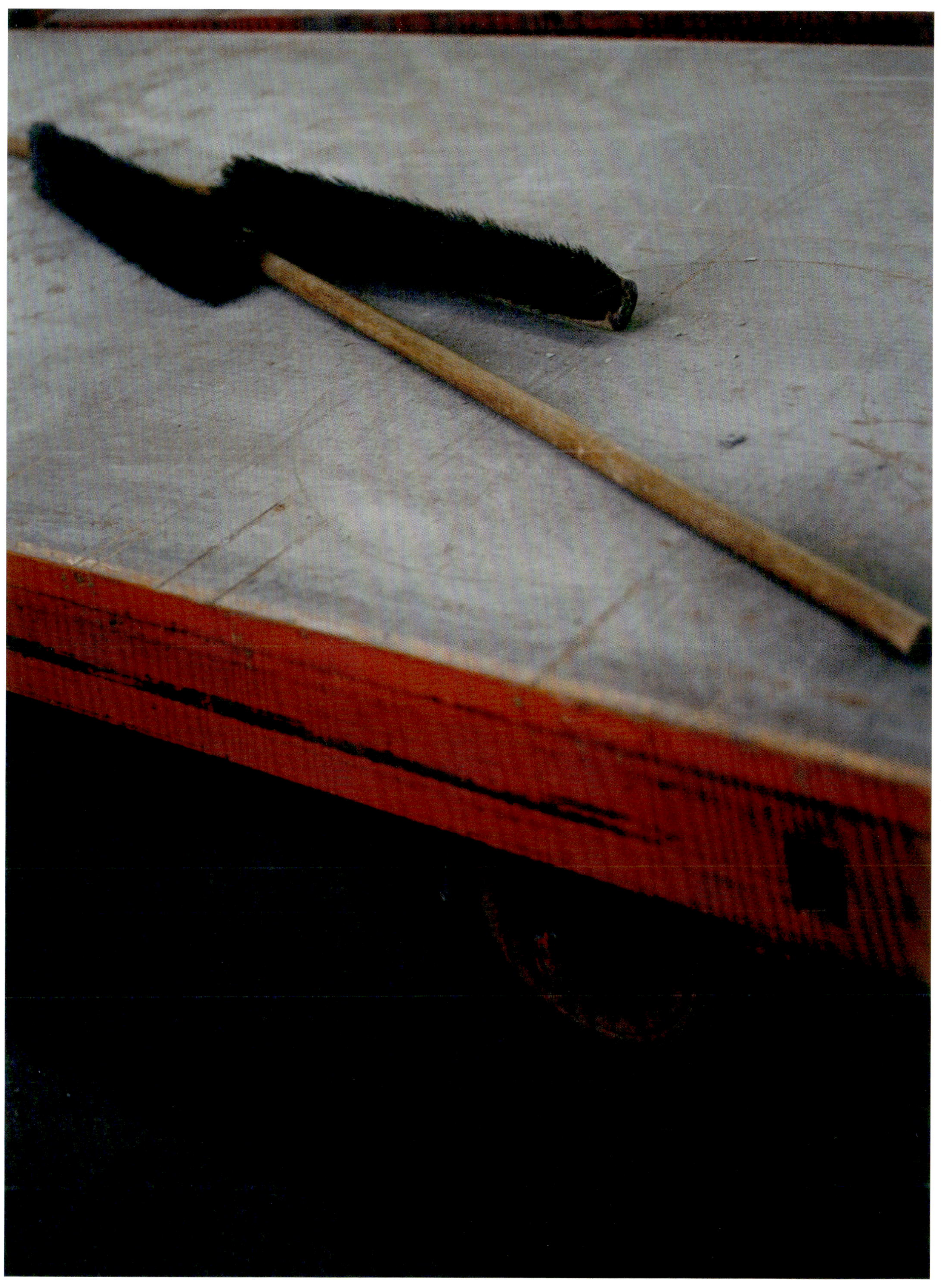

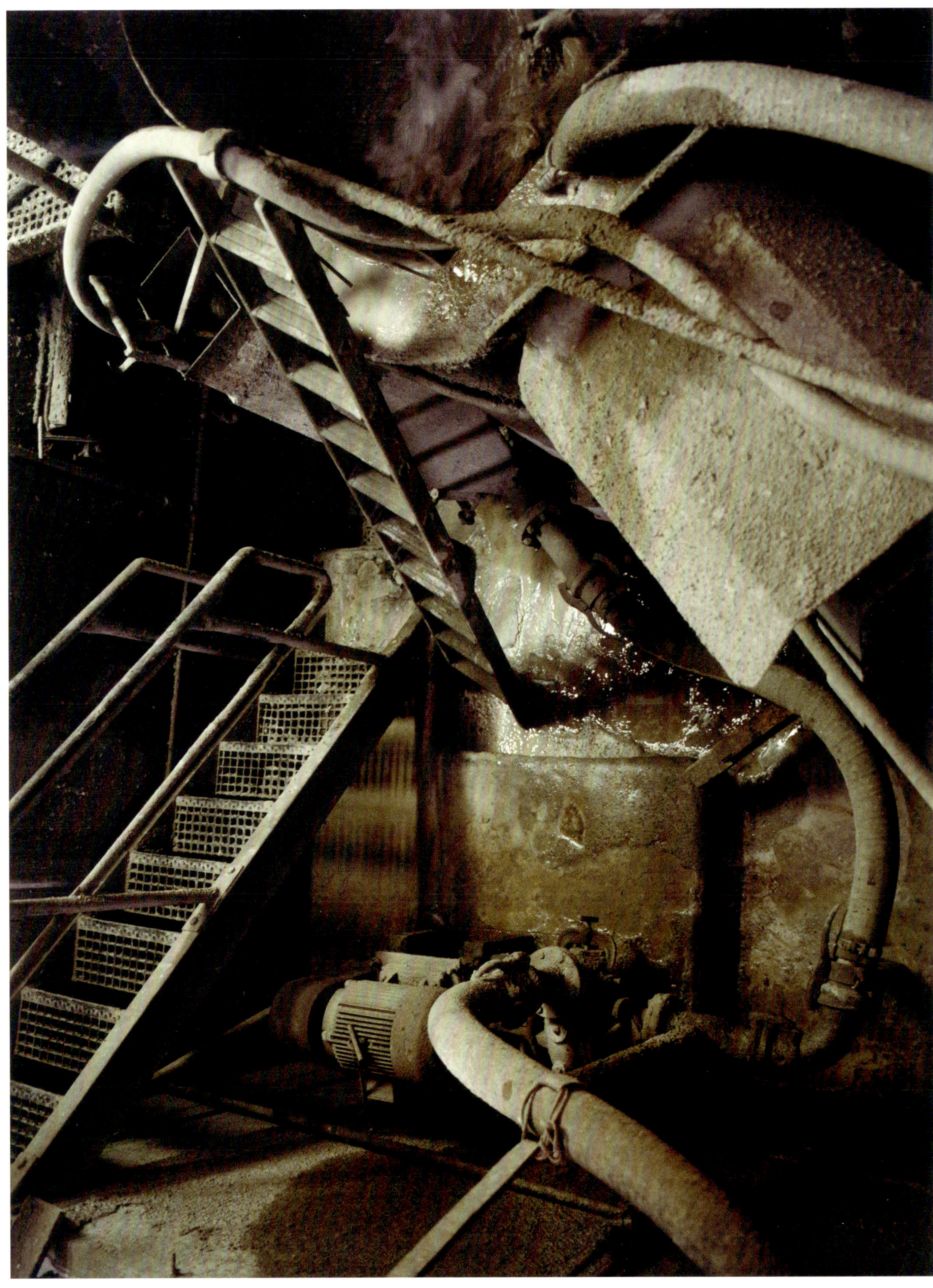

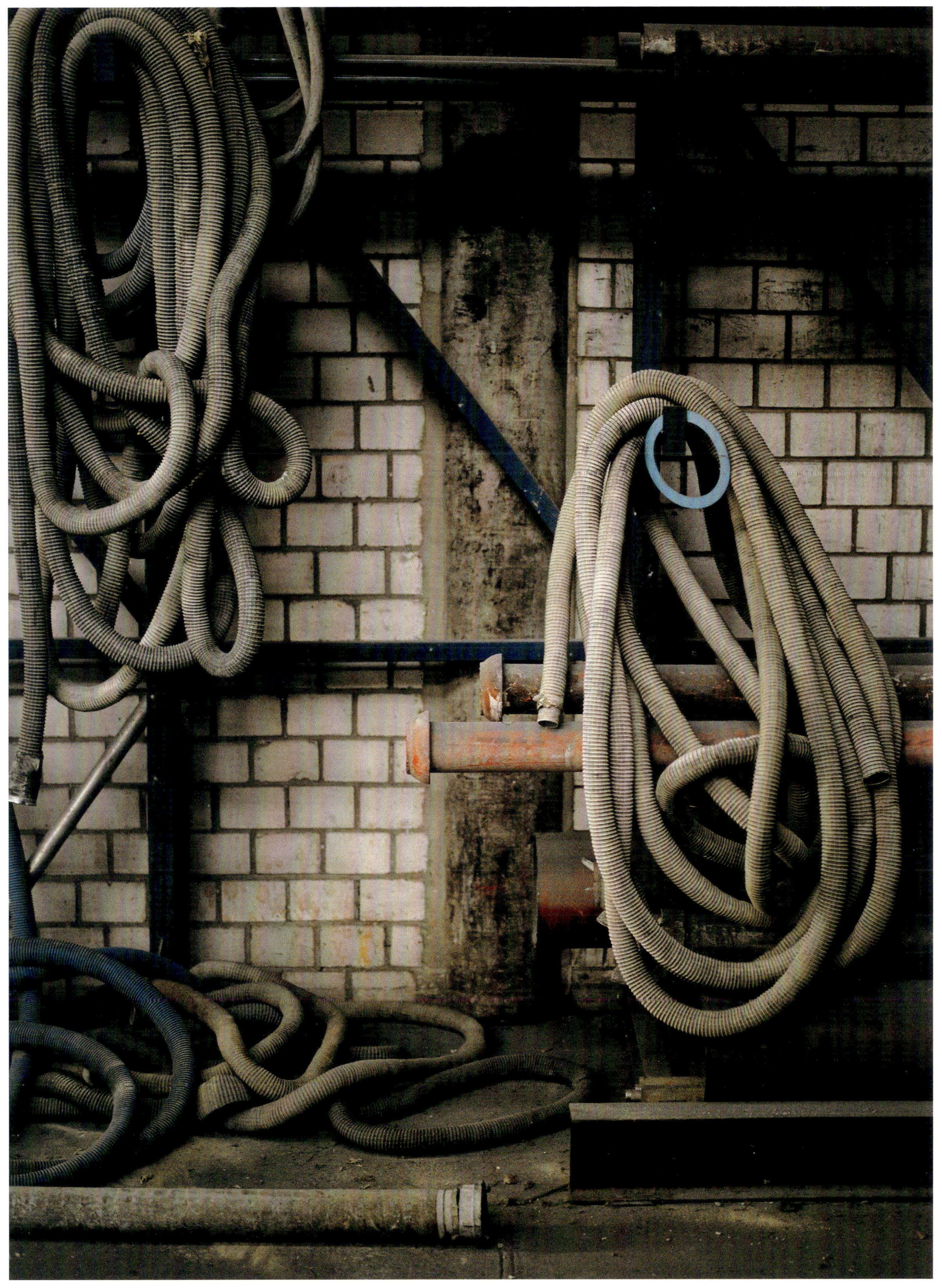

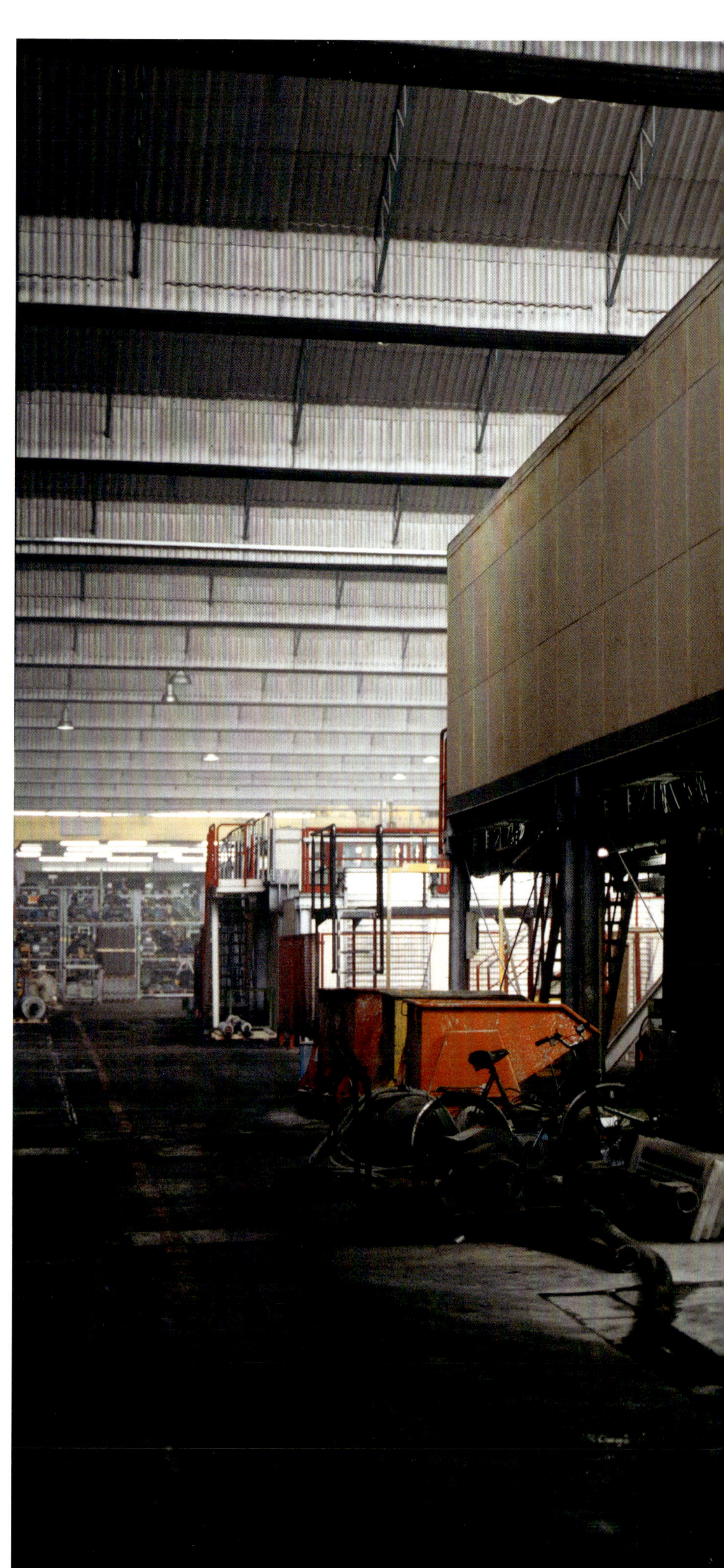

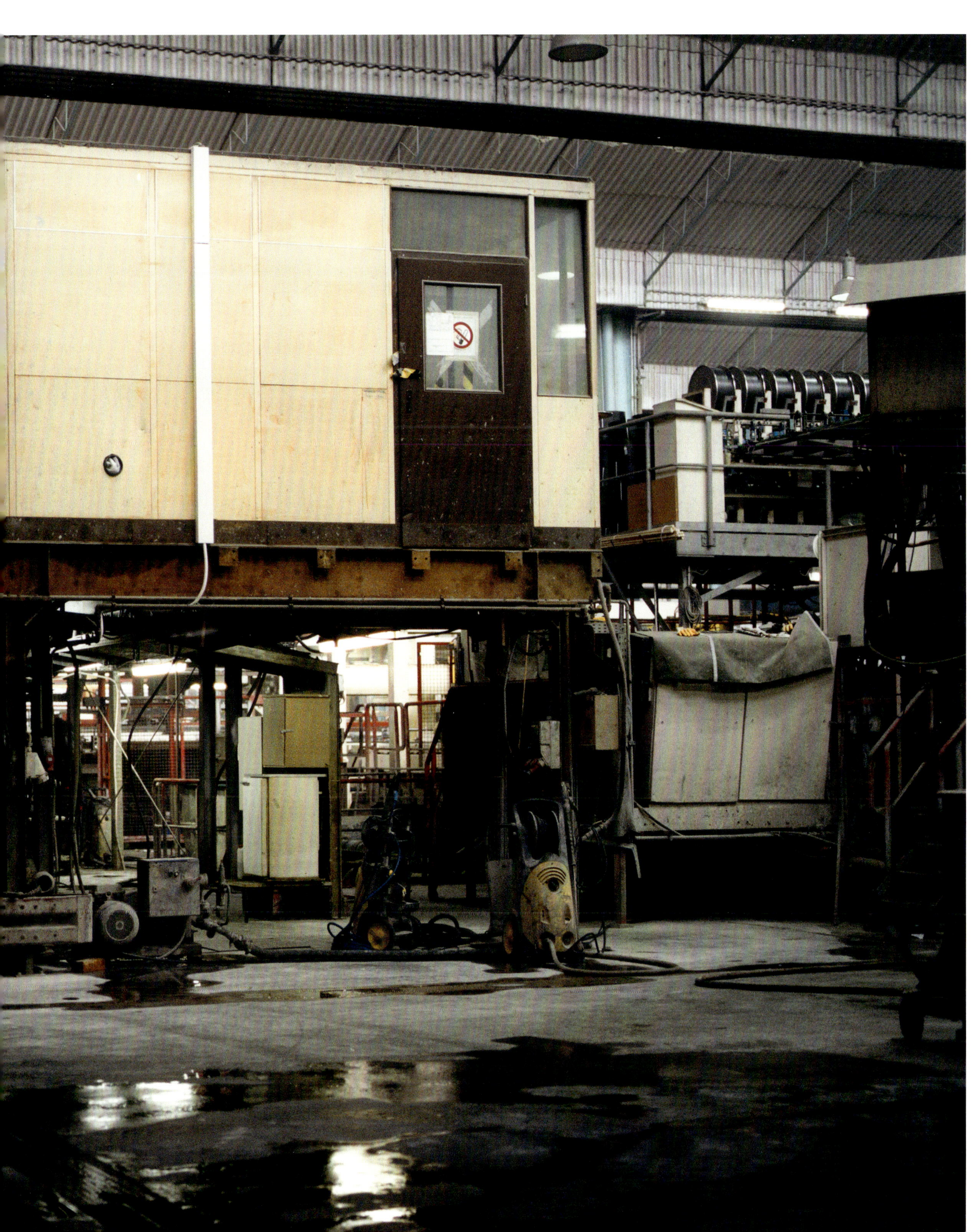

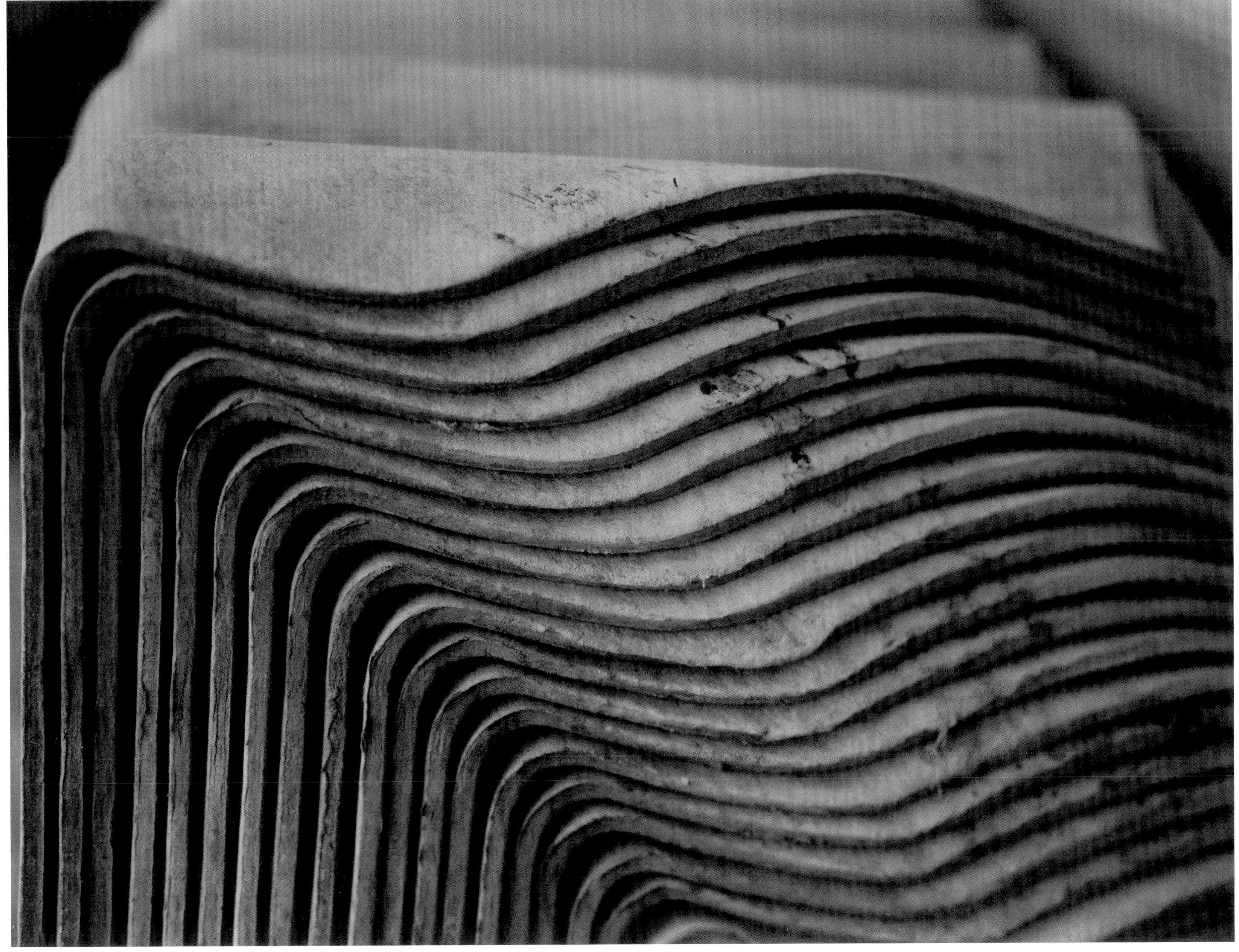

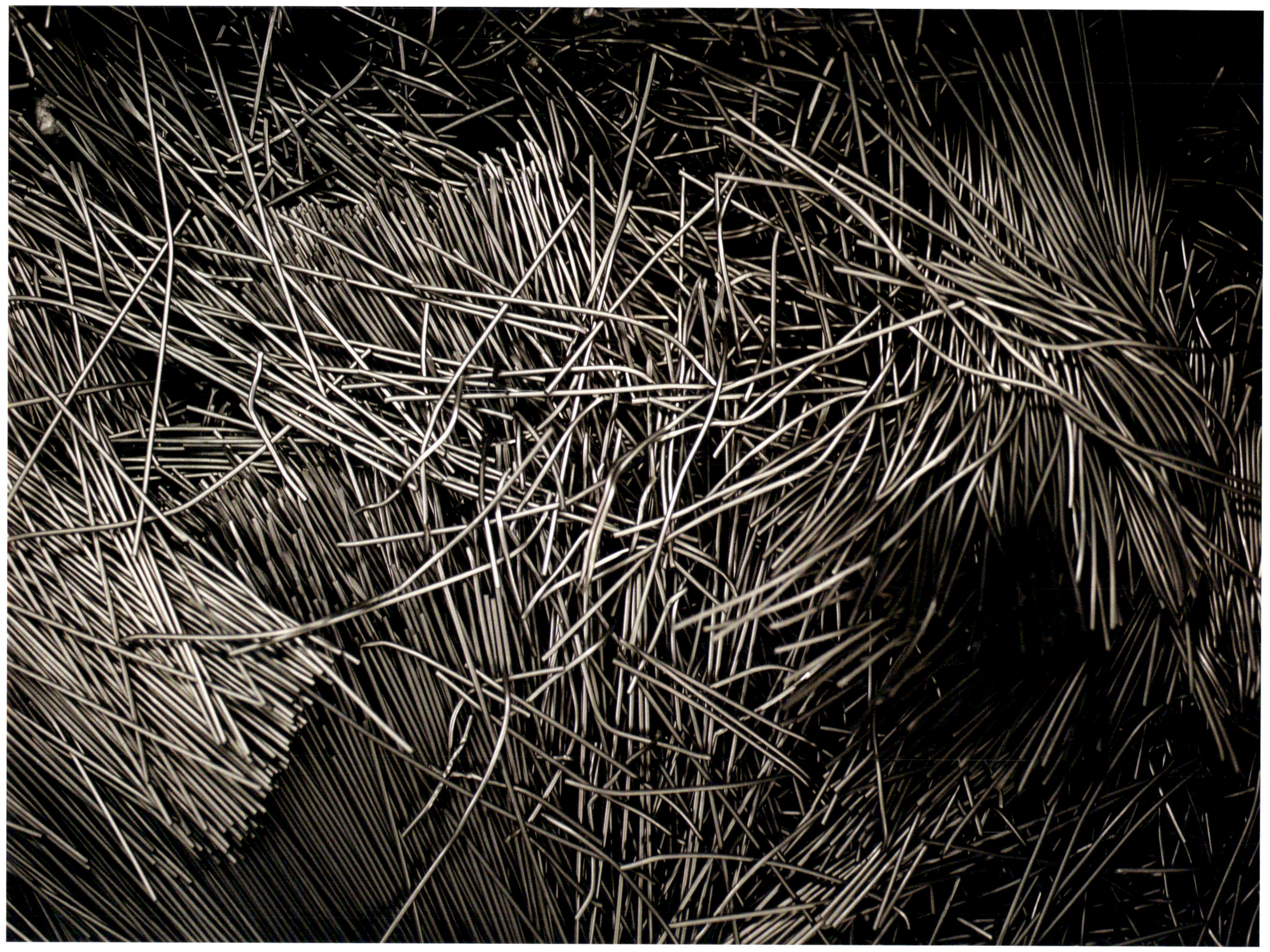

		Faber-Castell

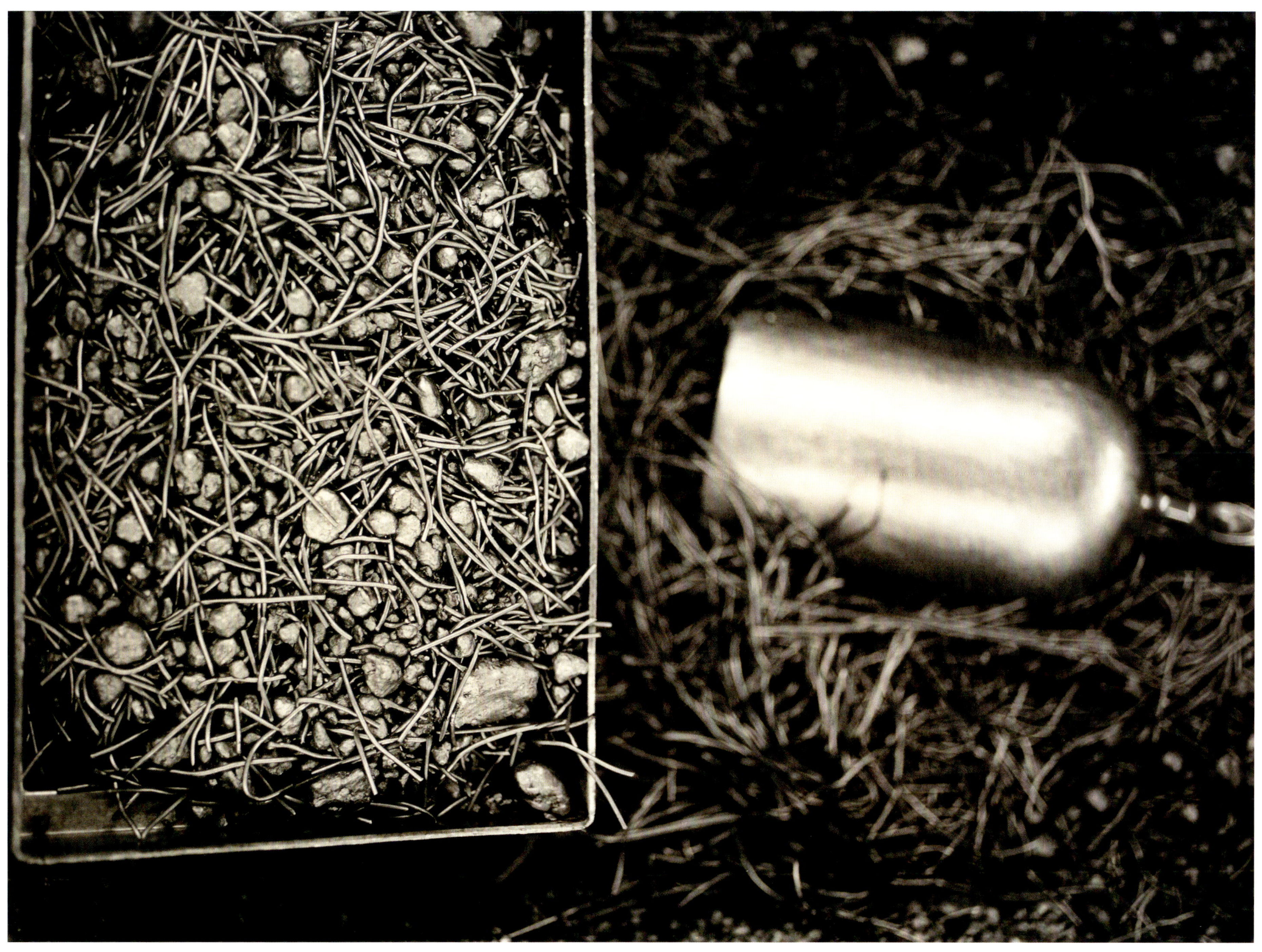

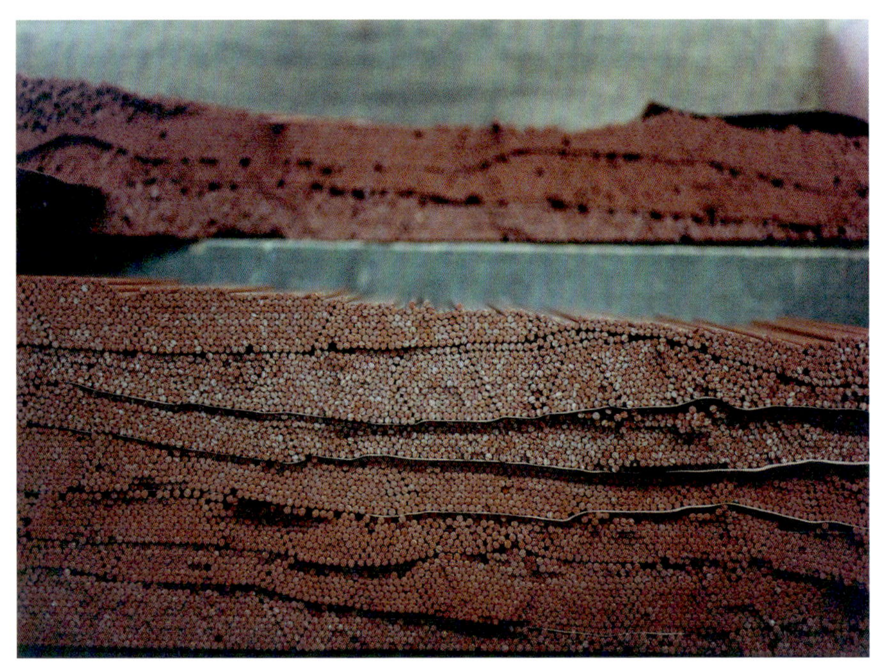
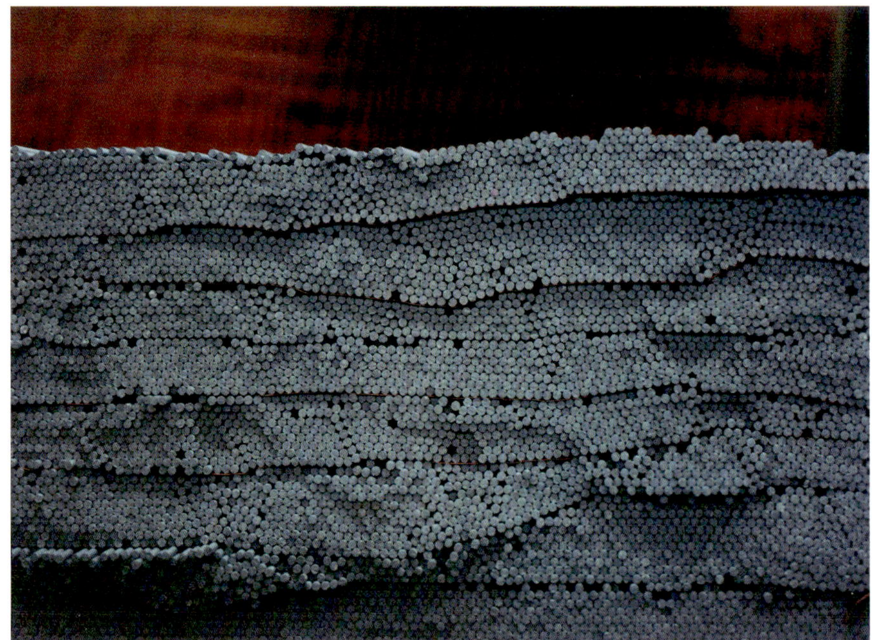

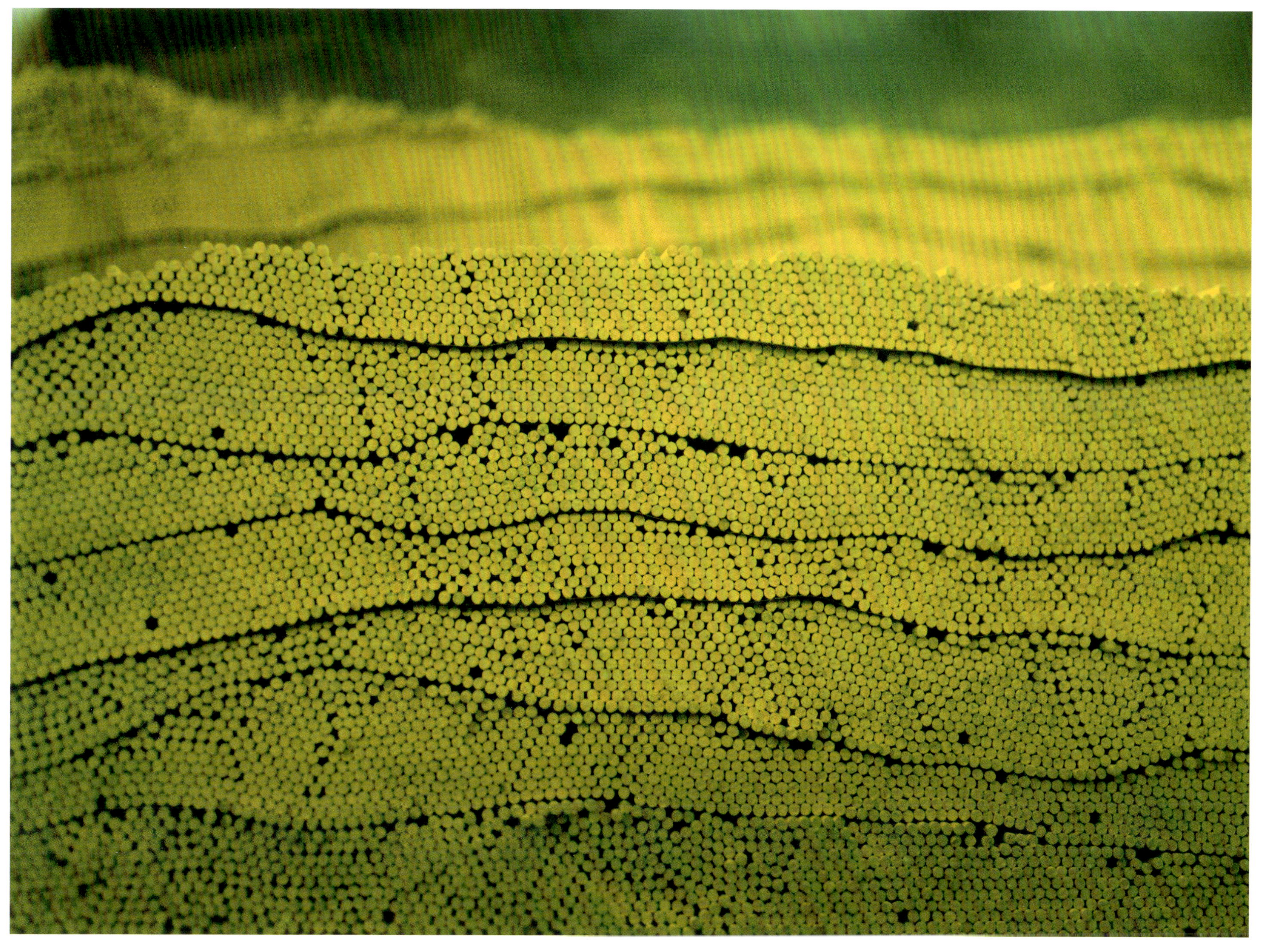

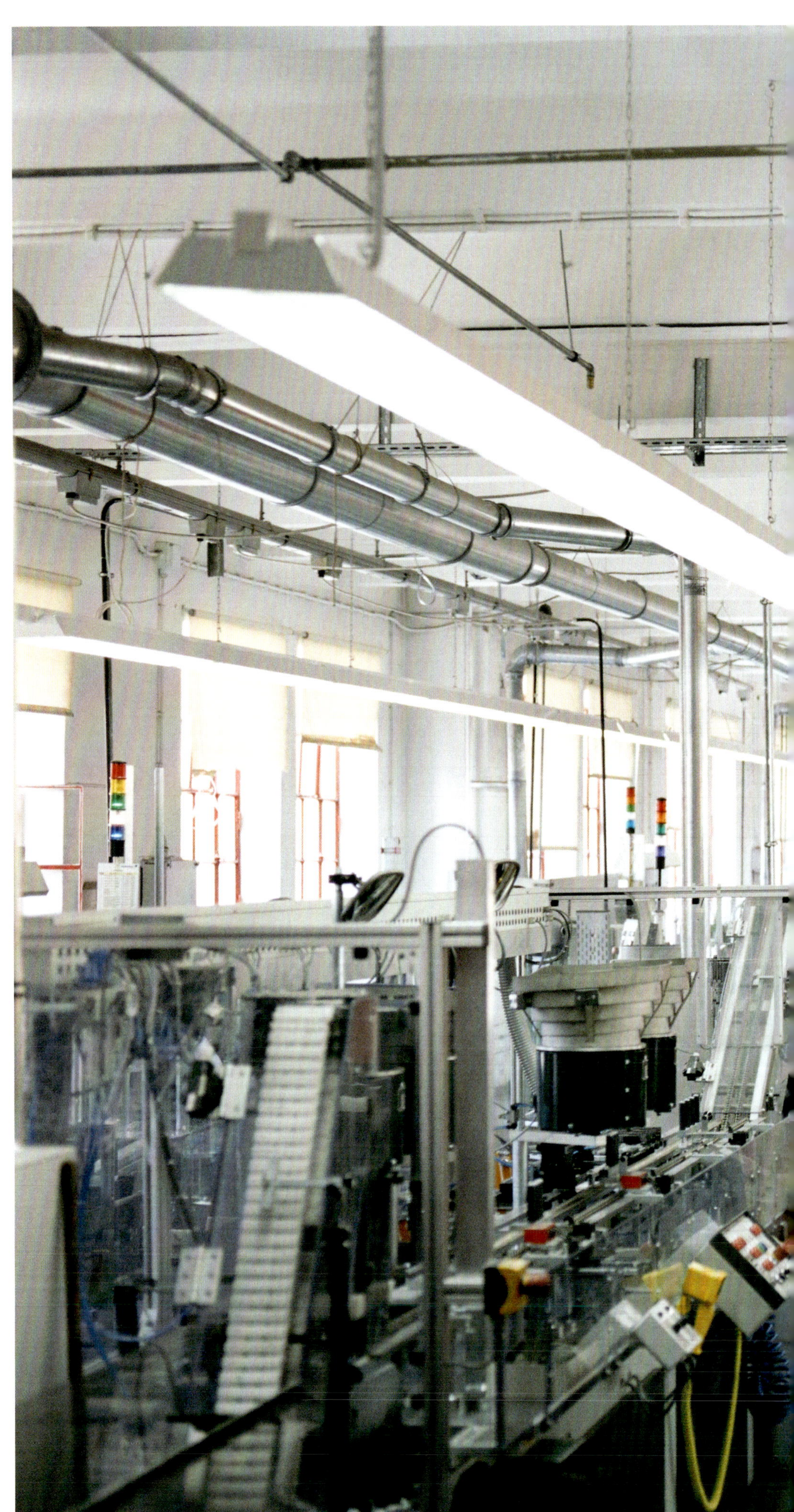

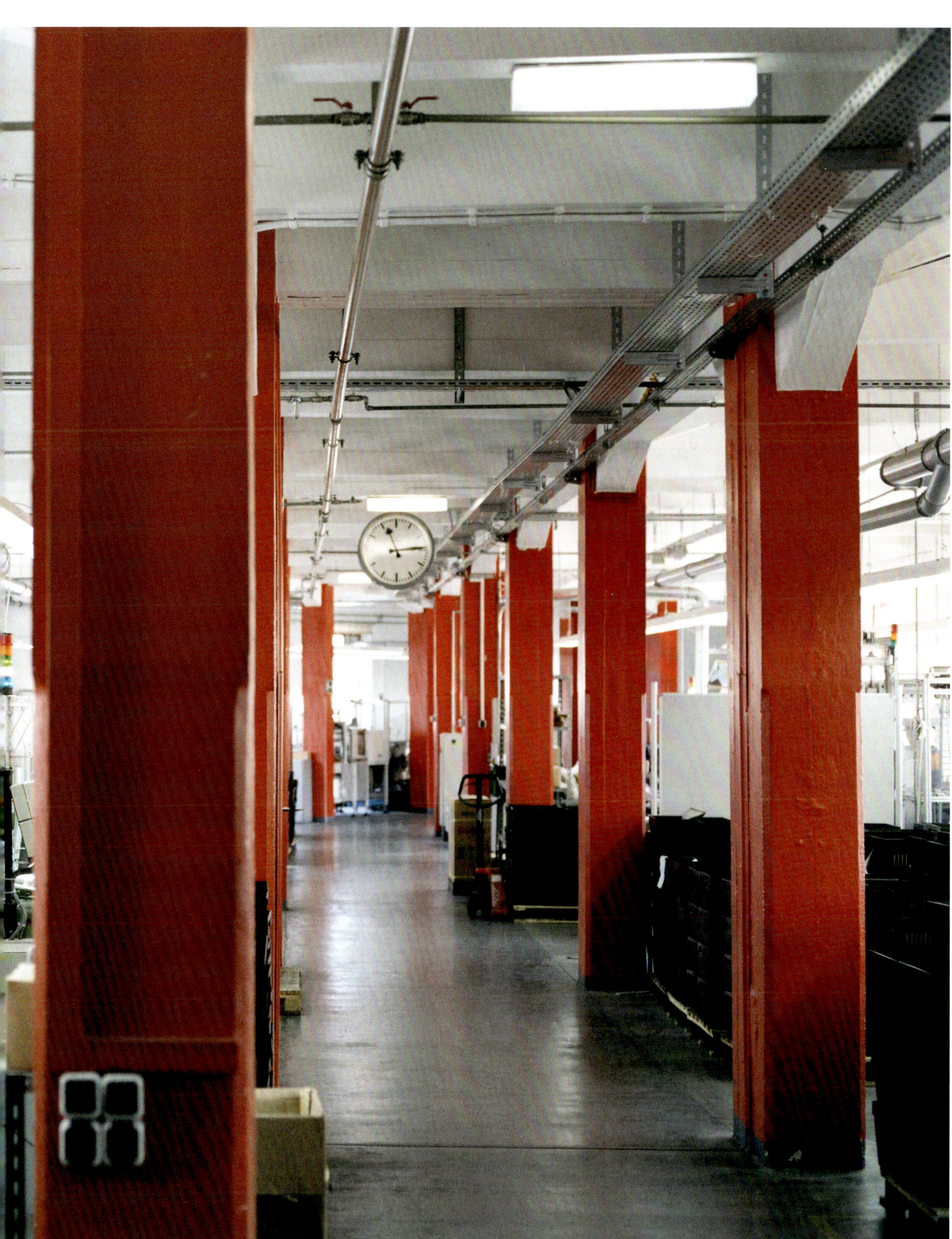

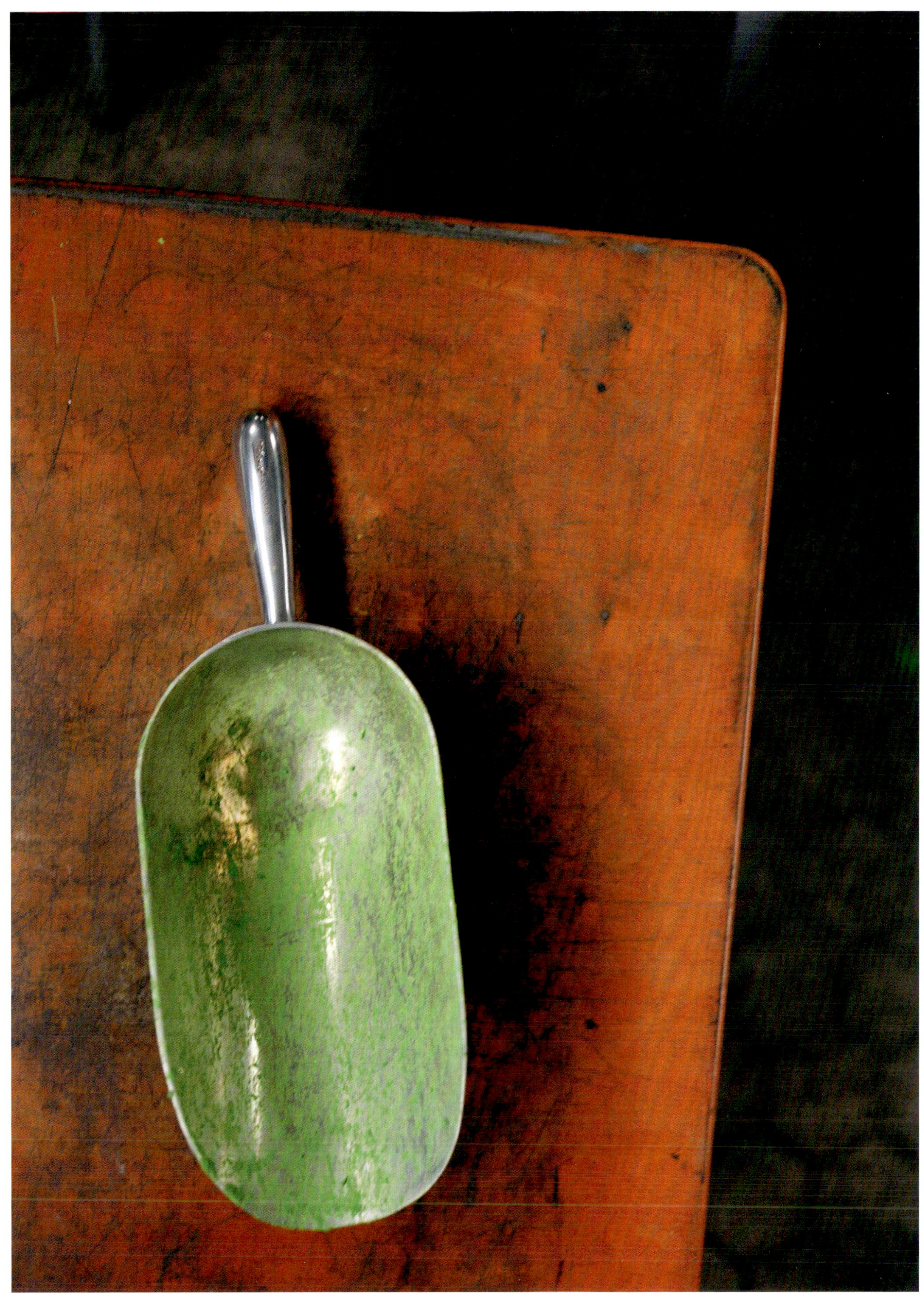

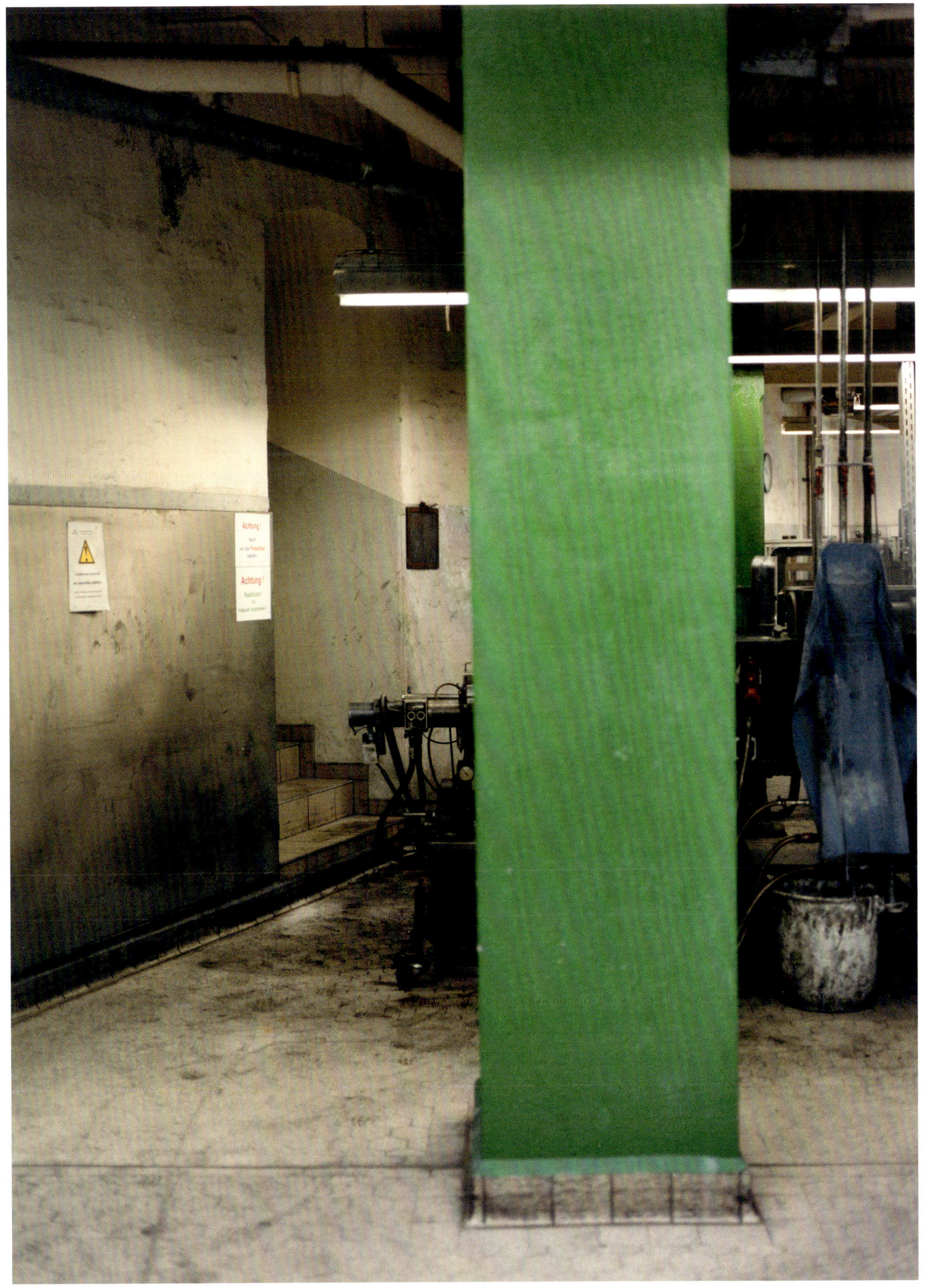

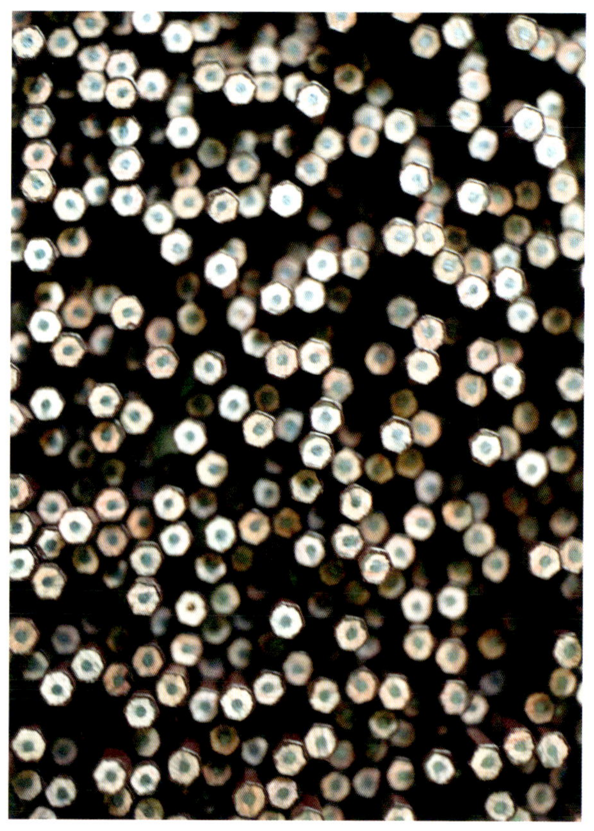
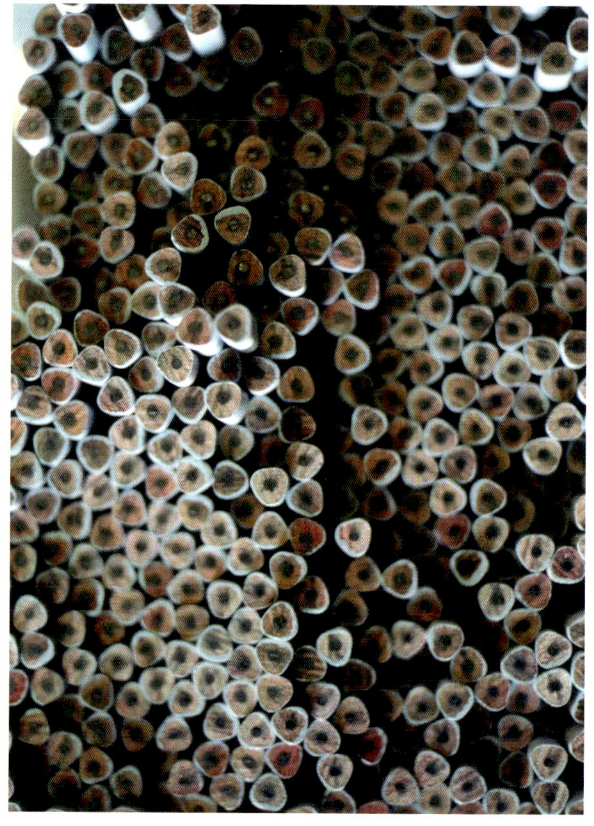

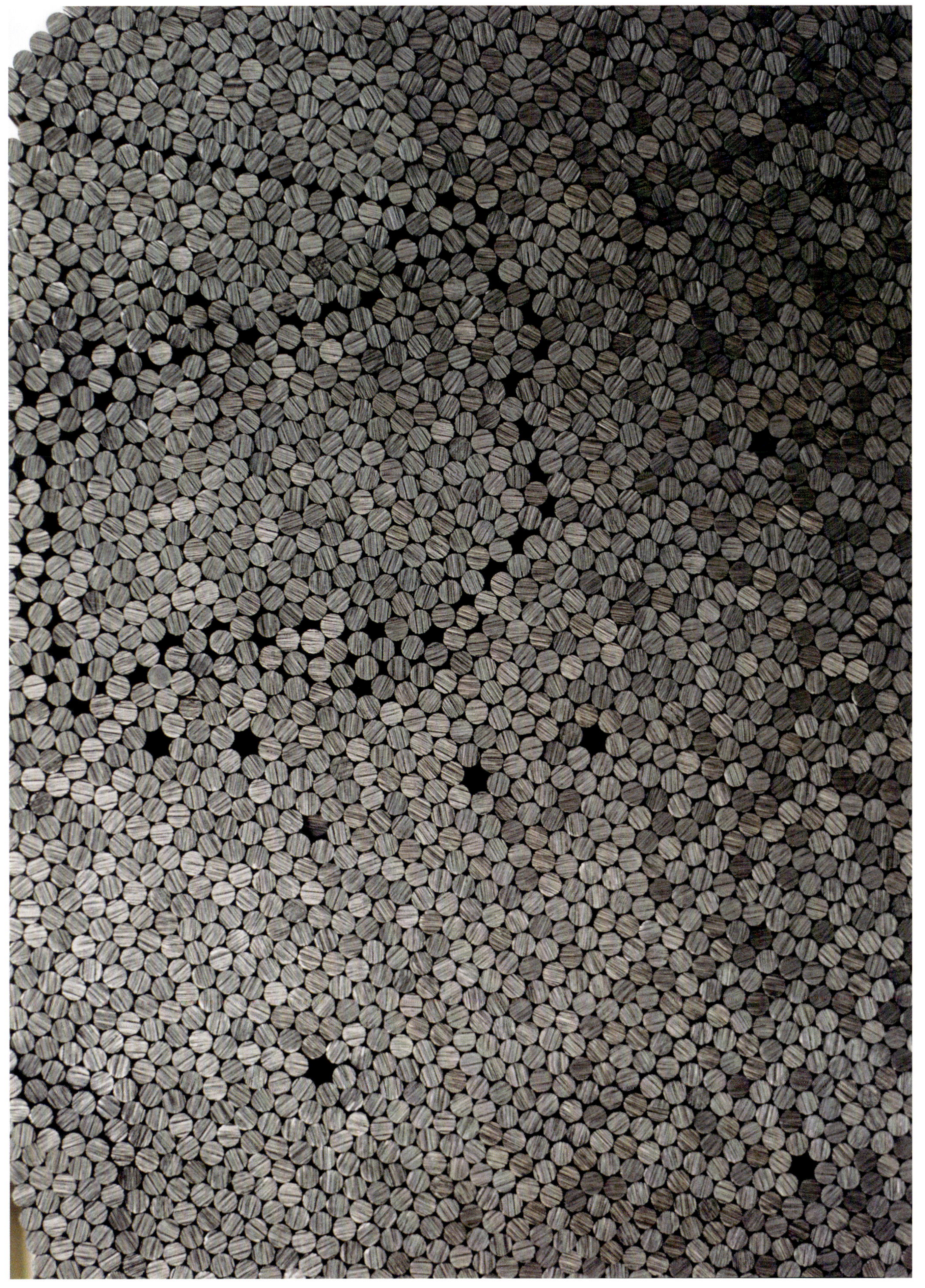

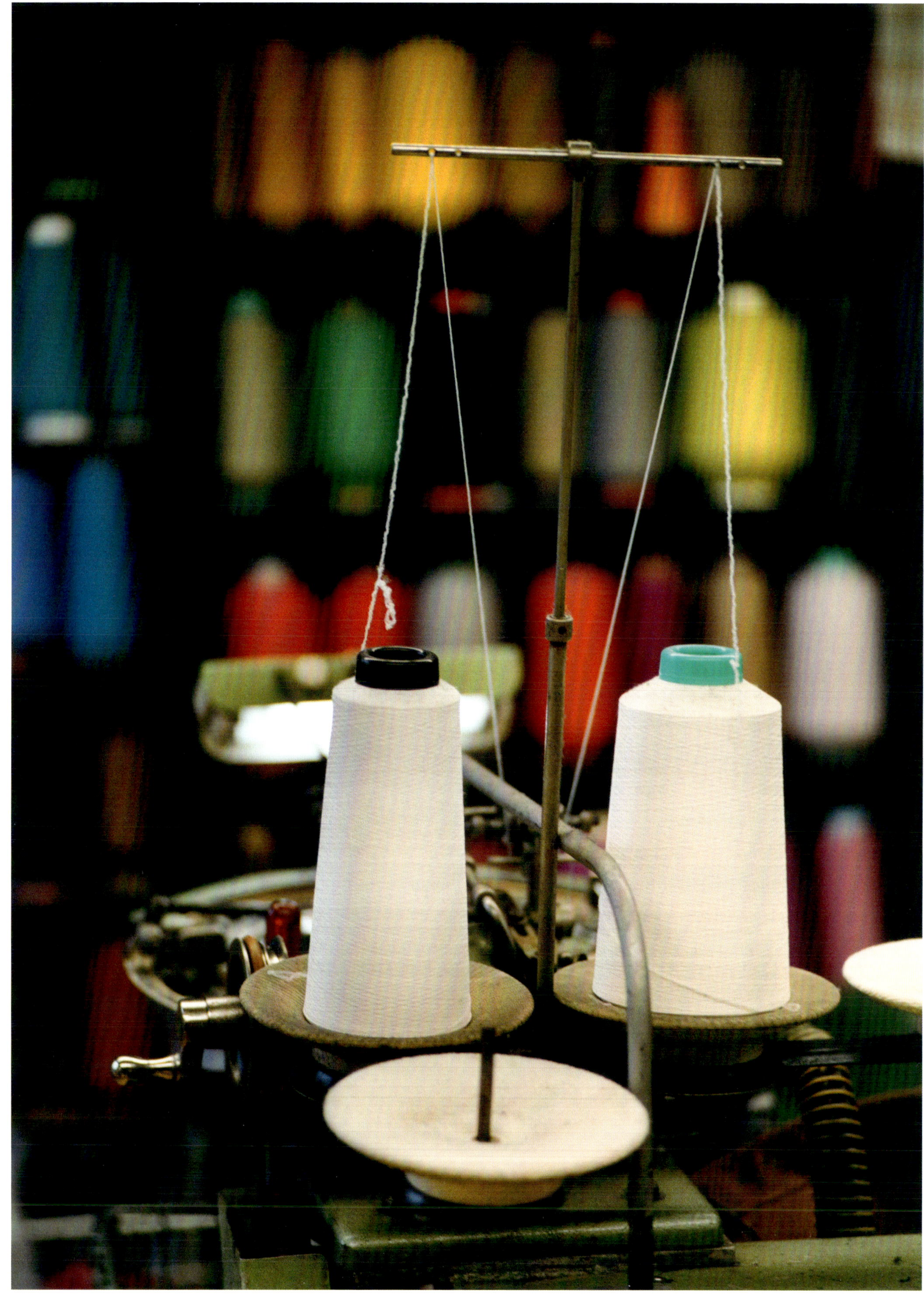

Falke

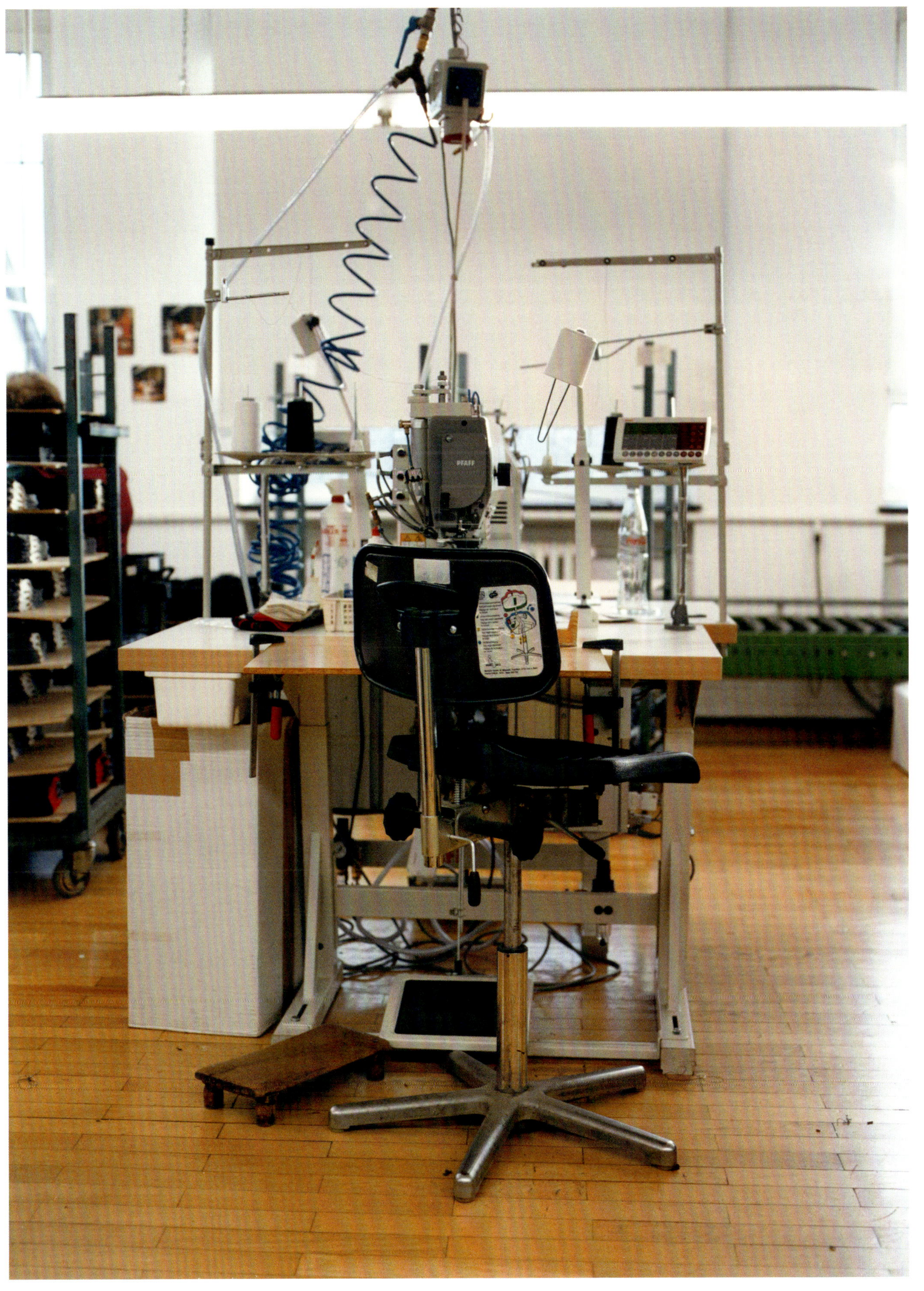

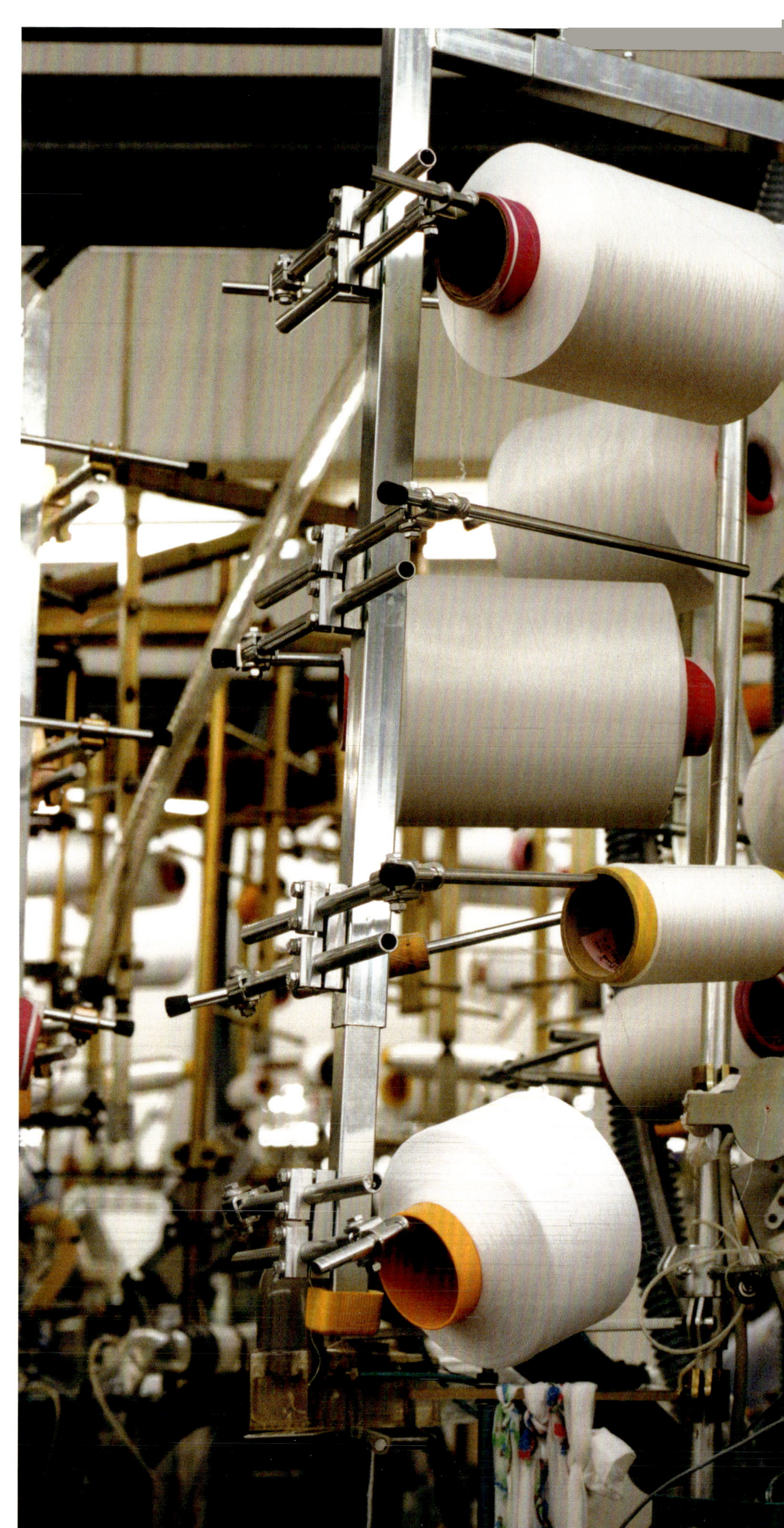

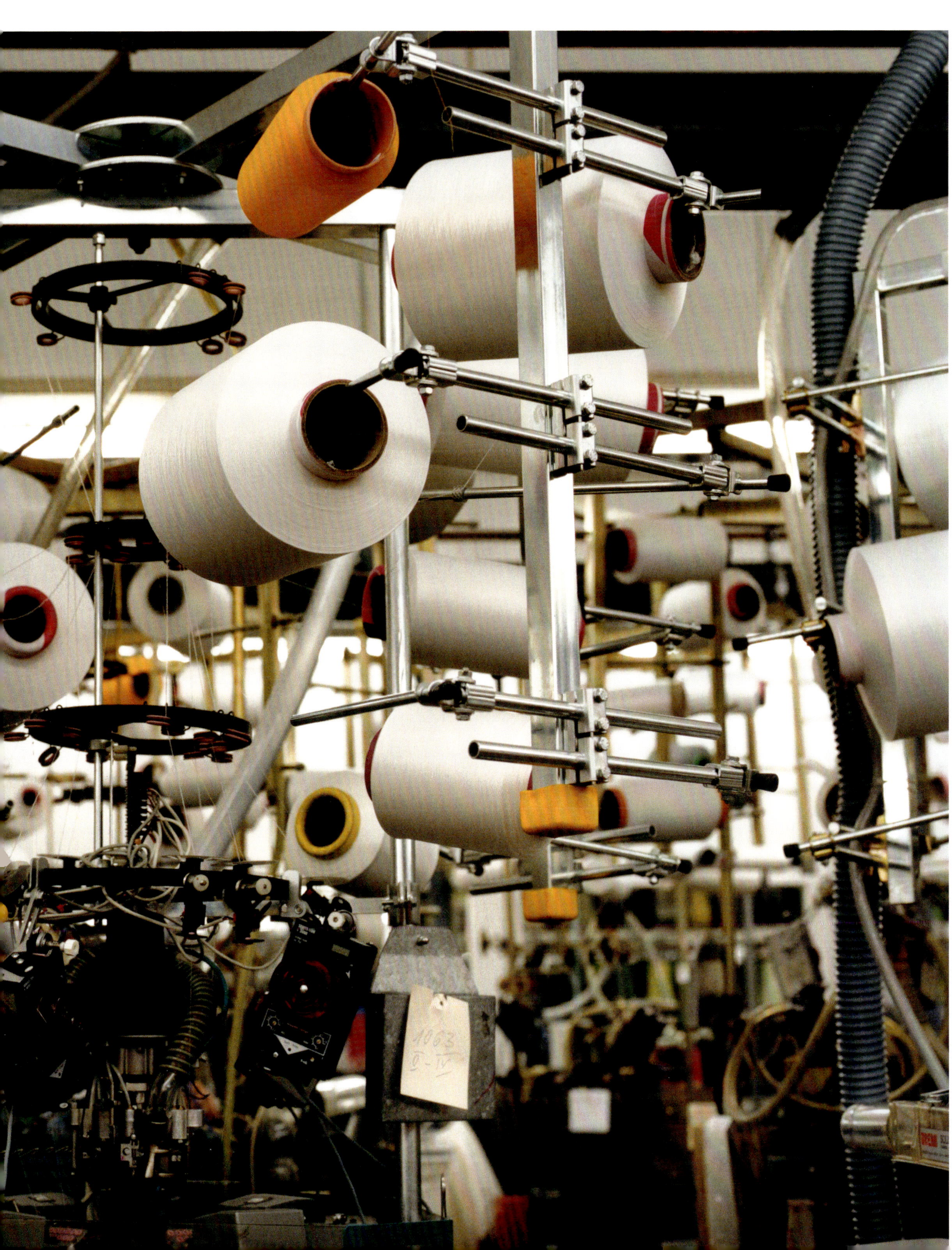

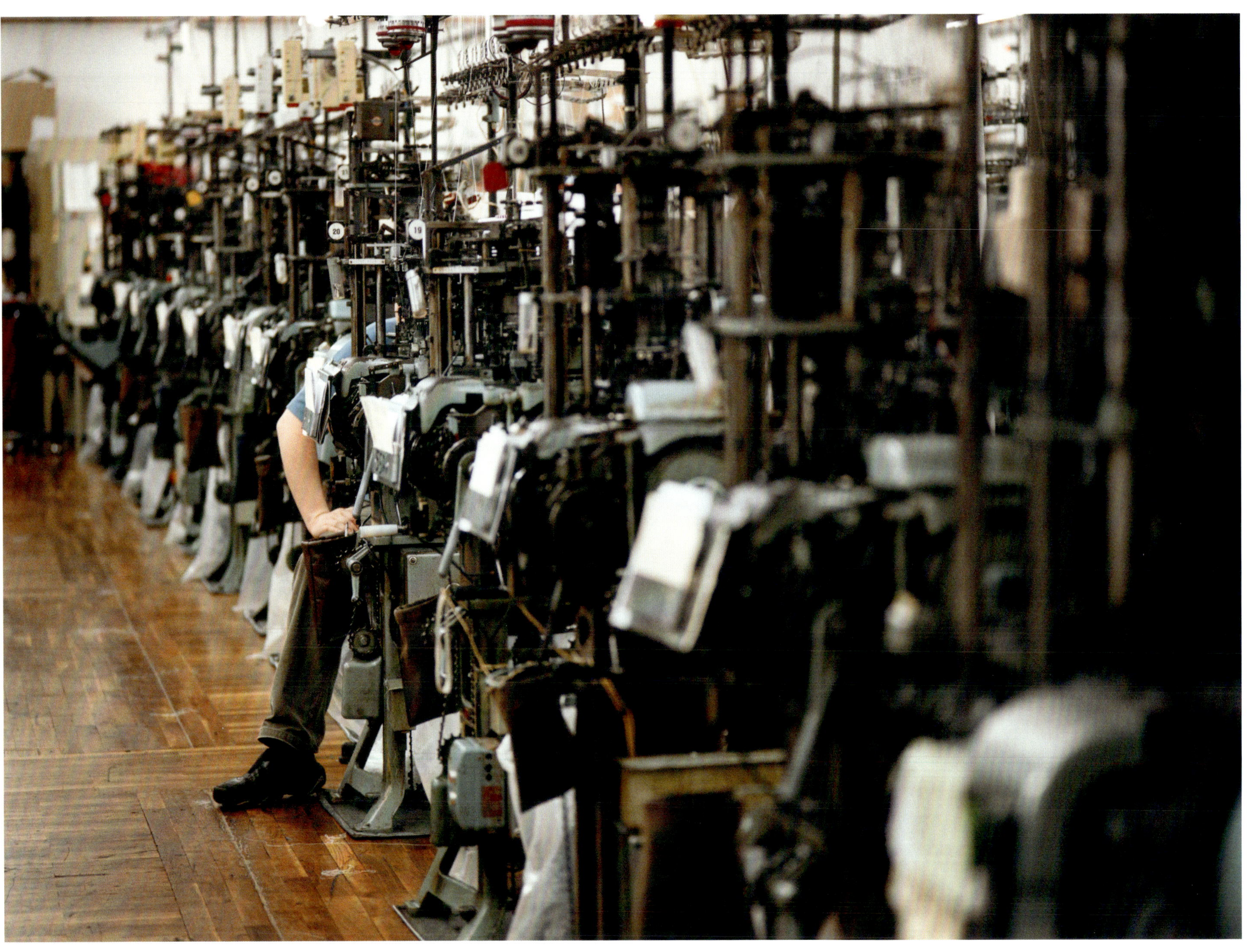

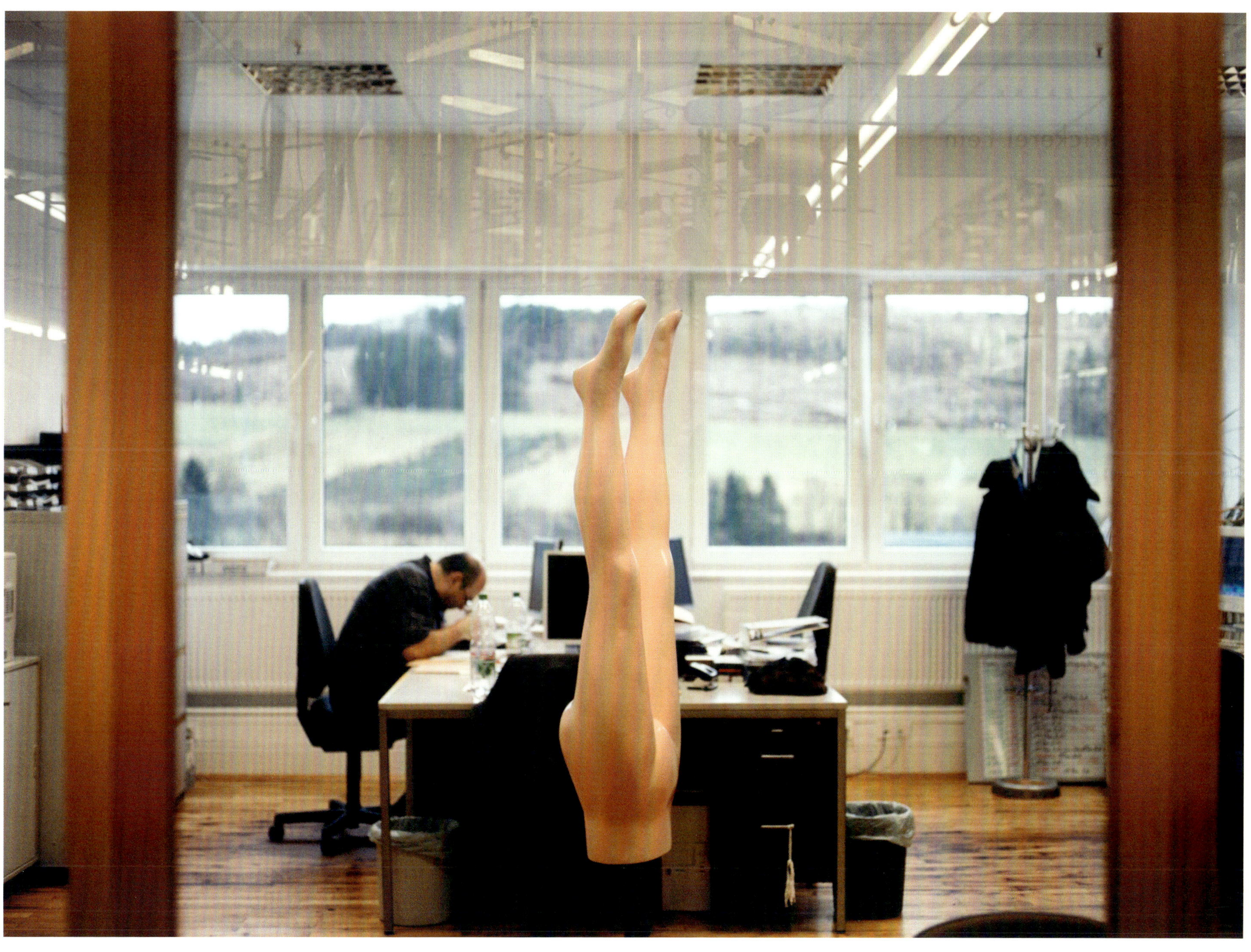

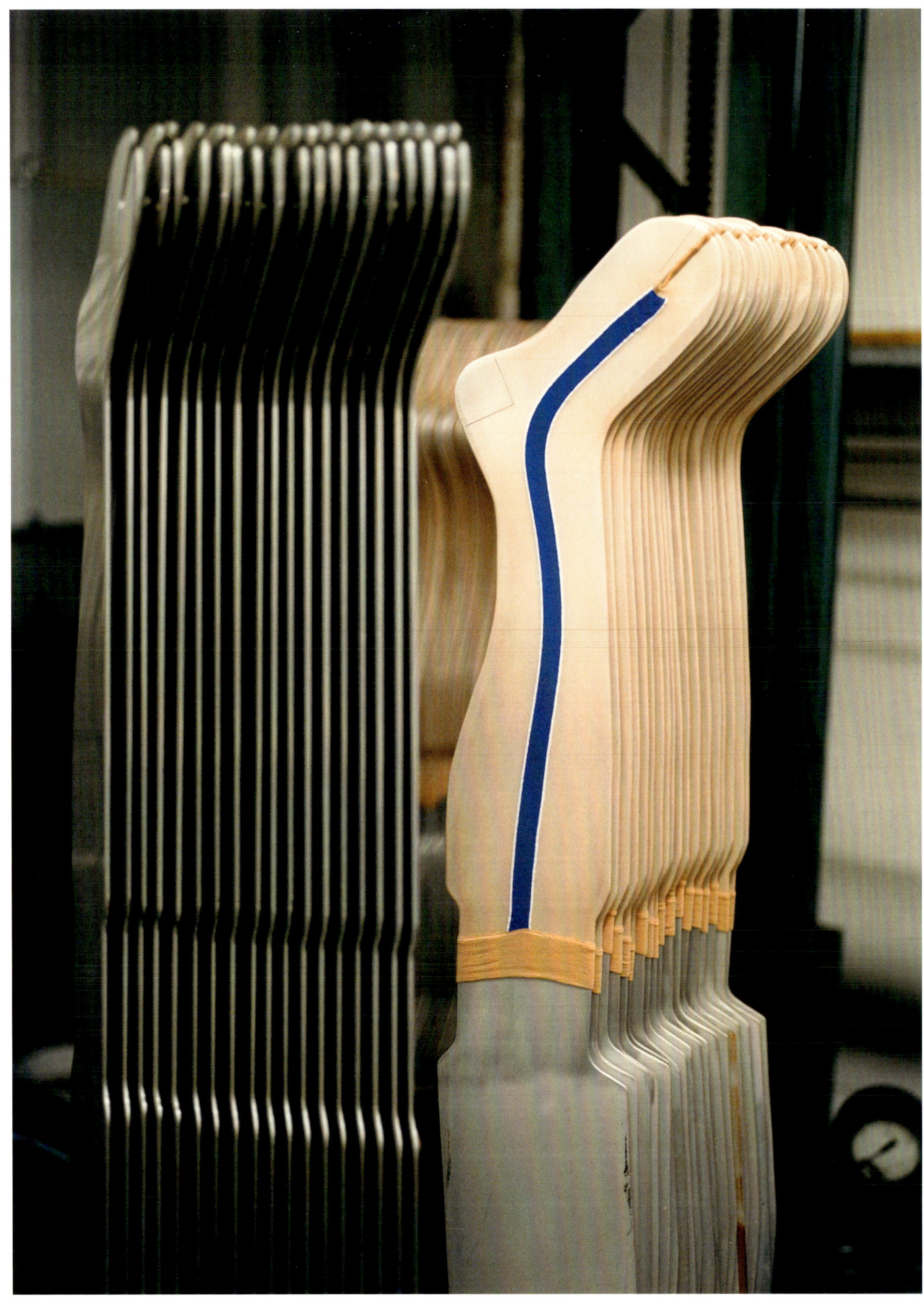

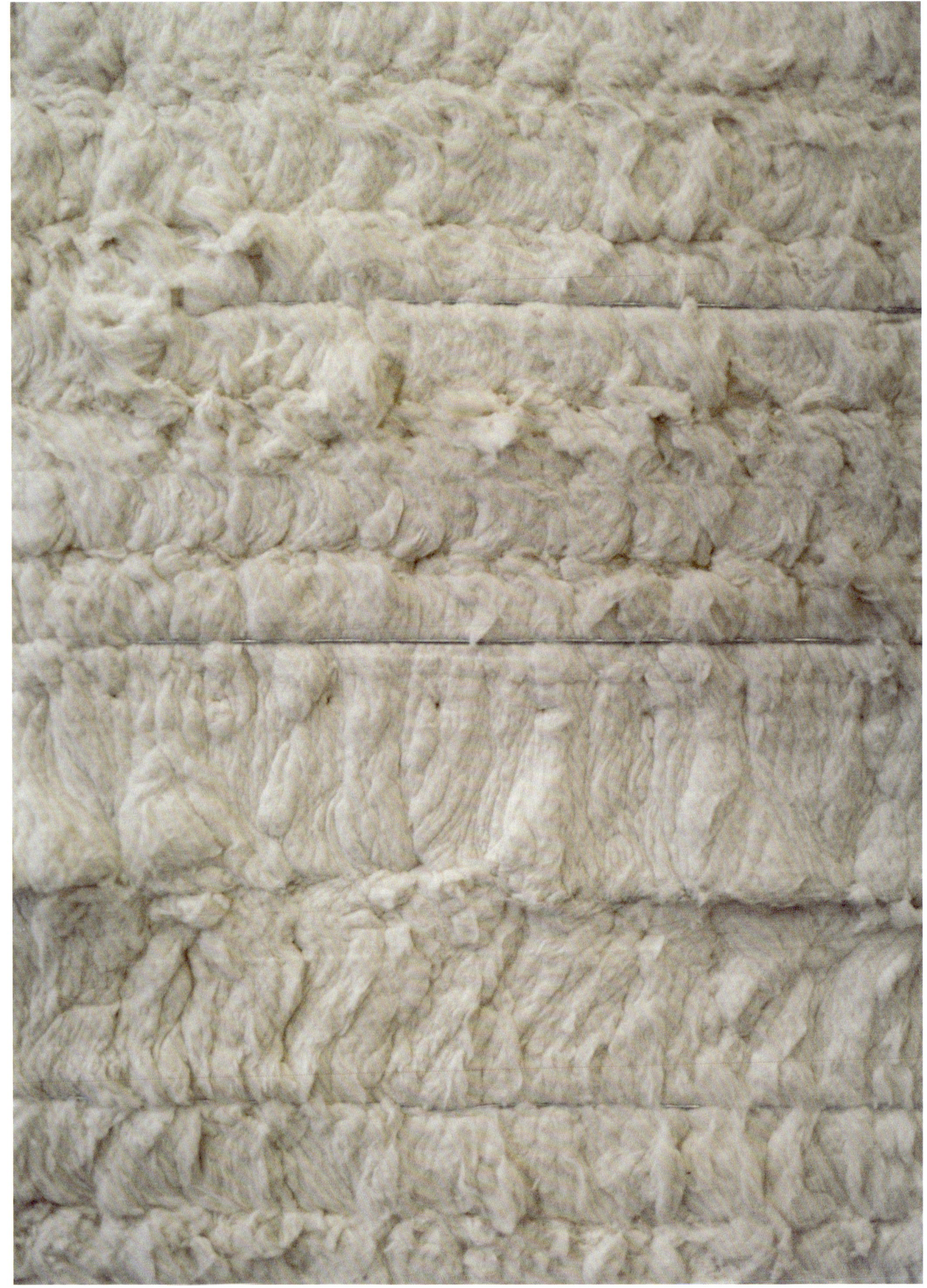

Giesecke & Devrient

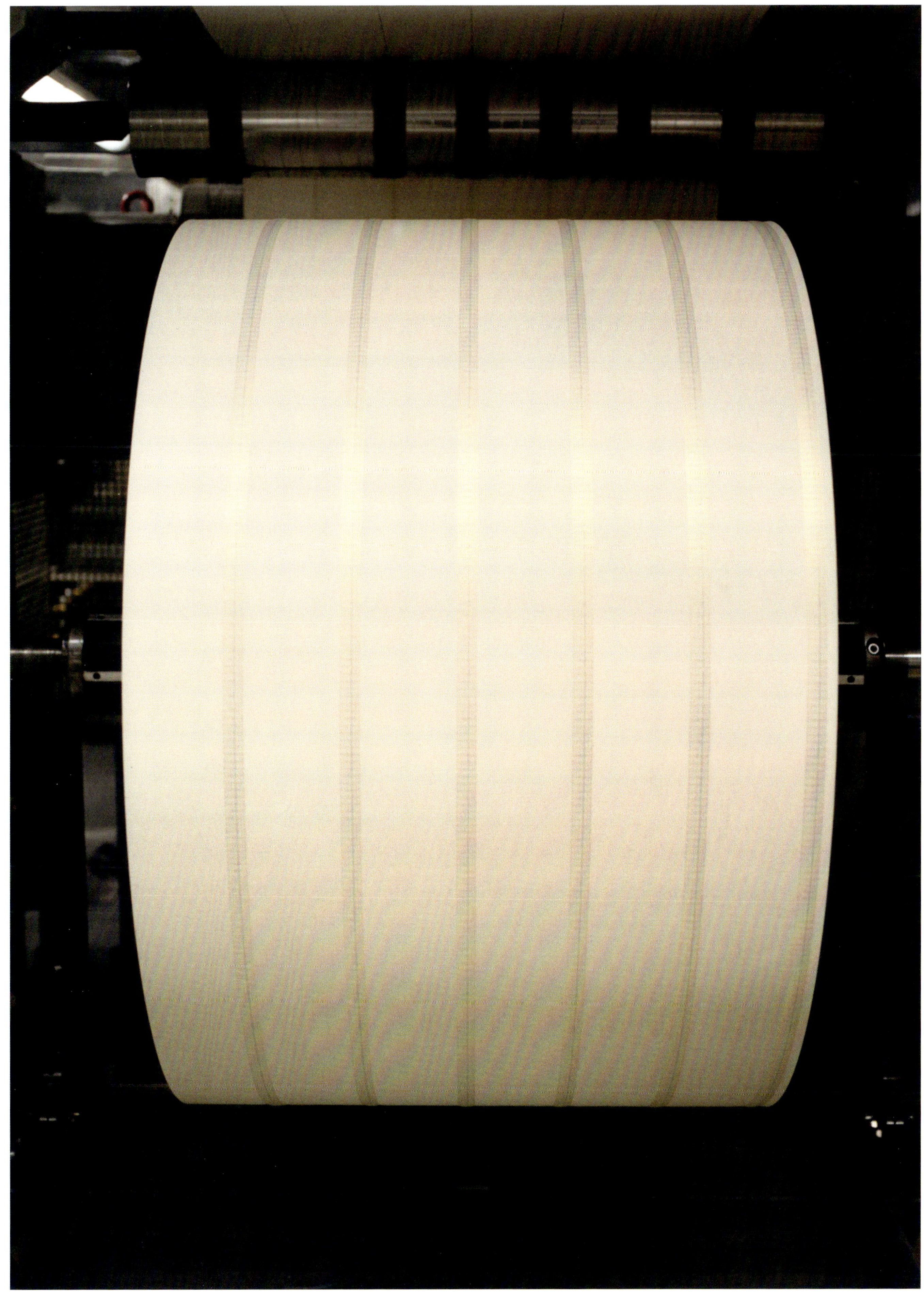

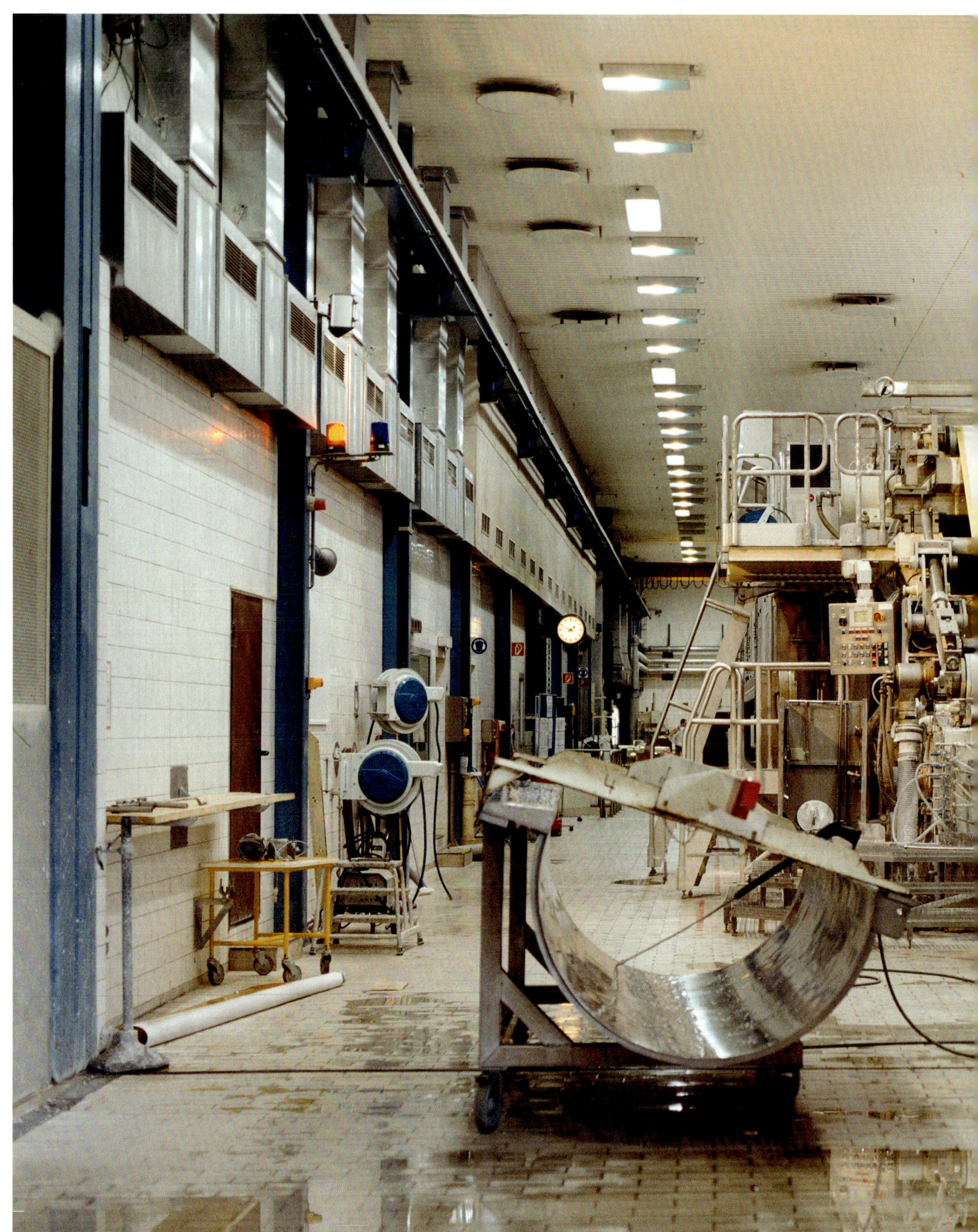

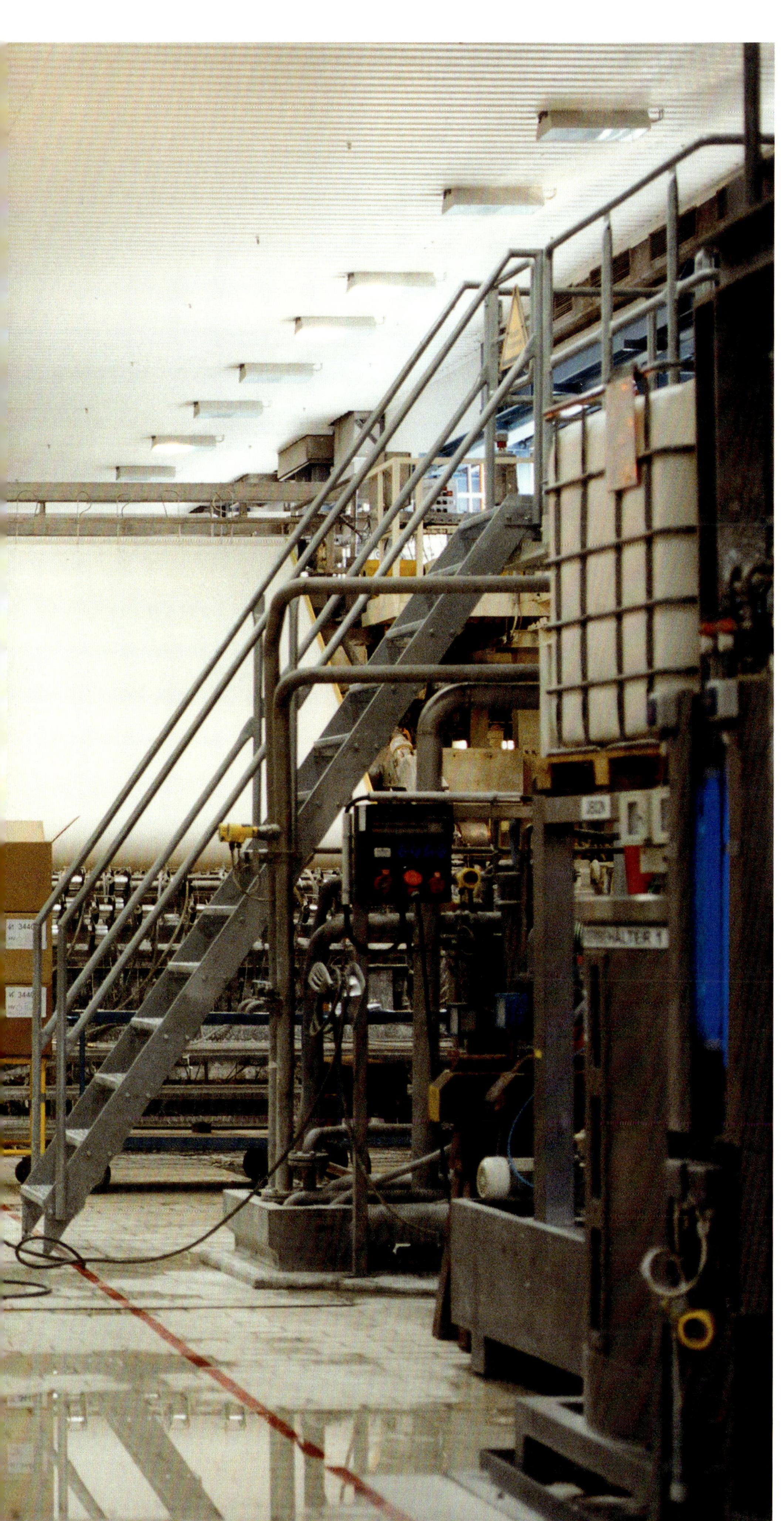

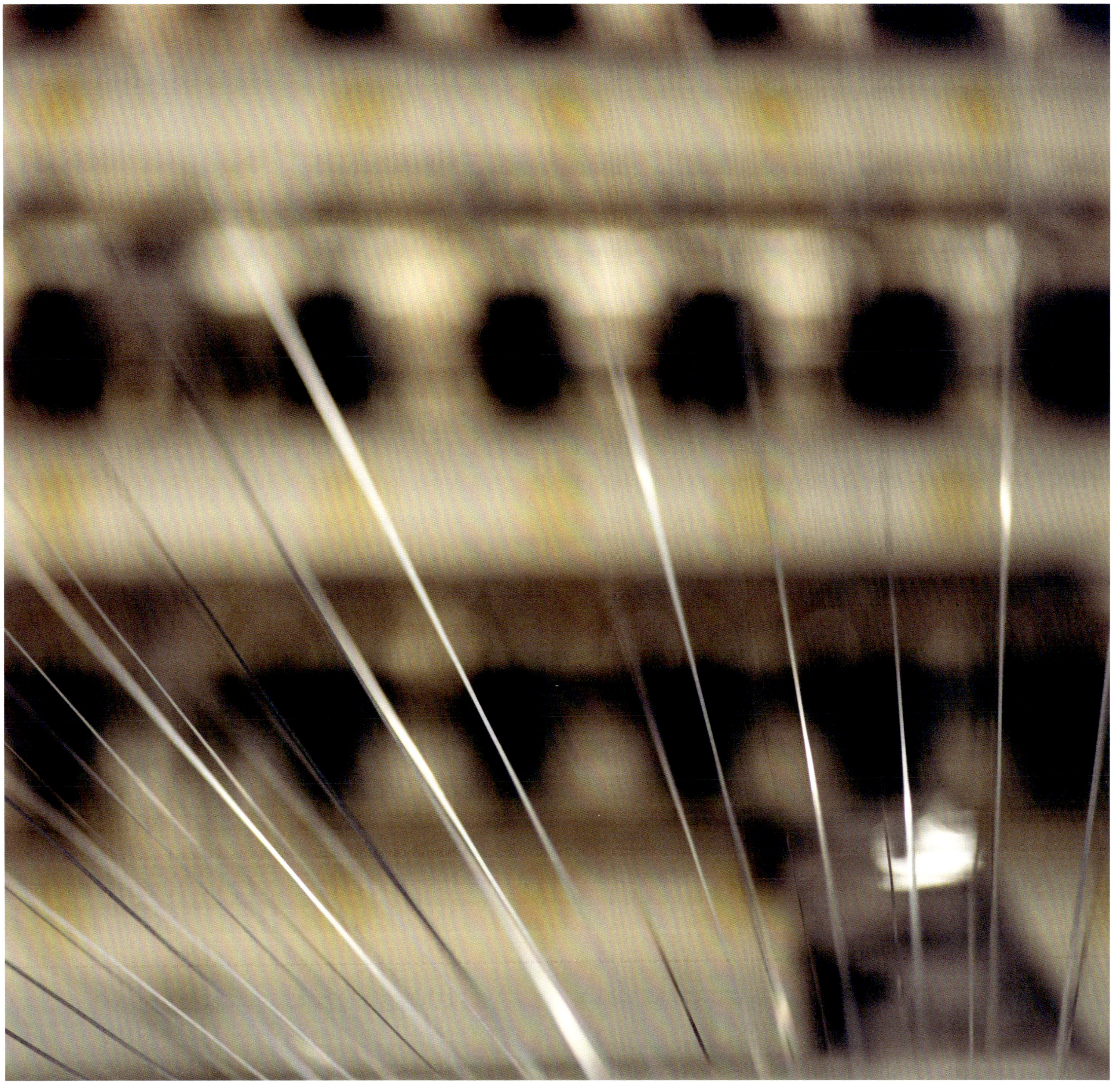

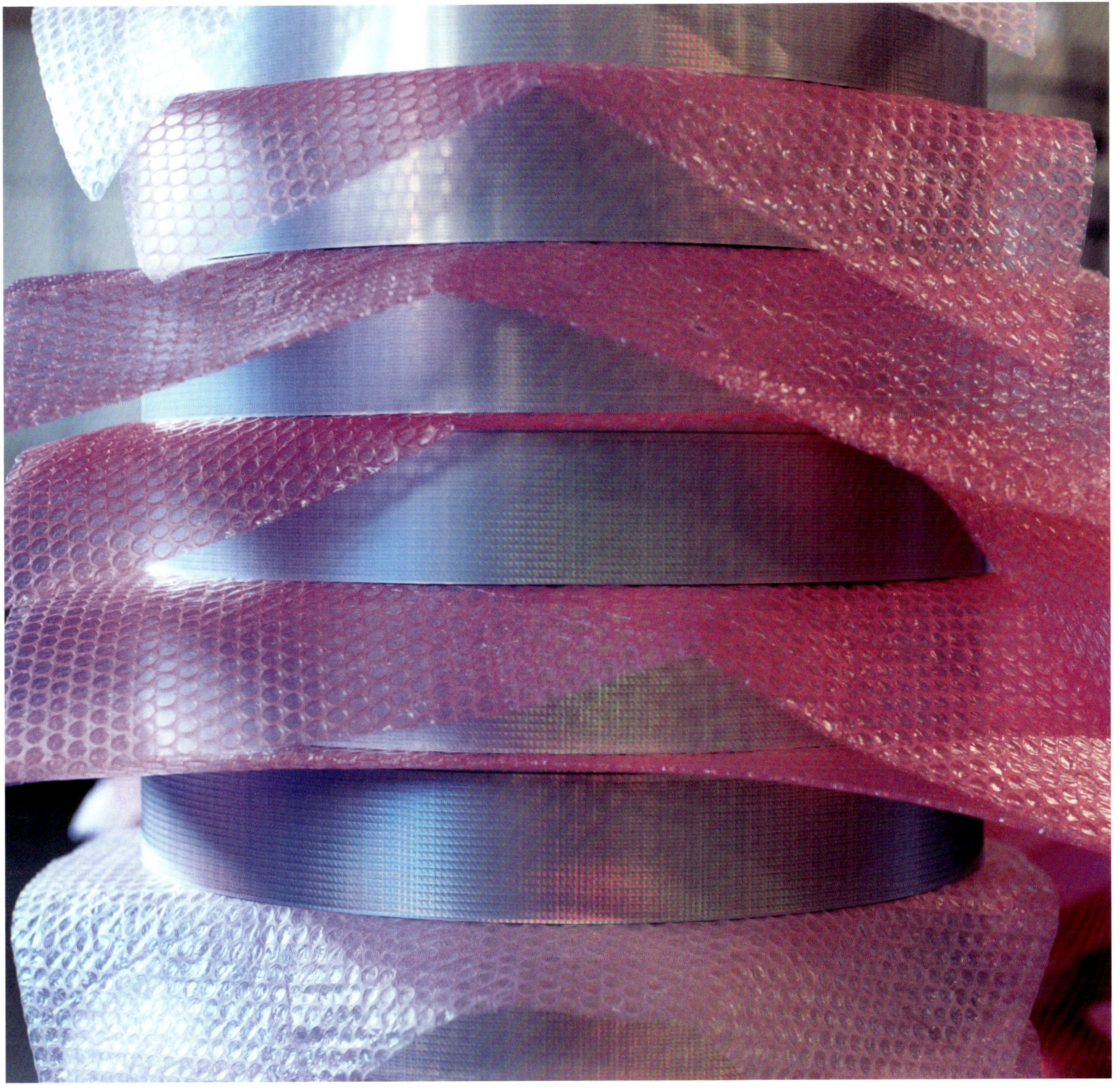

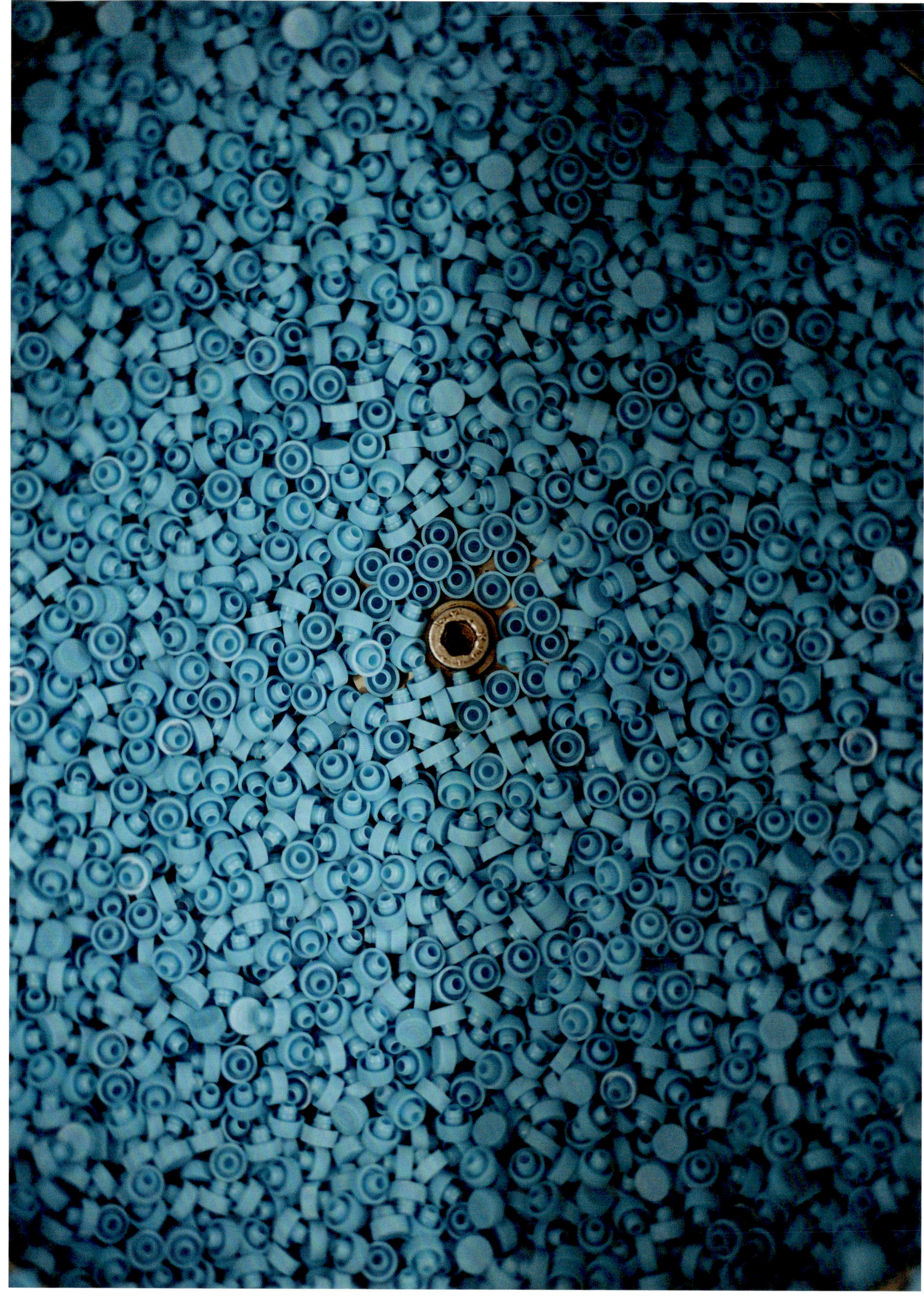

Dr. Oetker

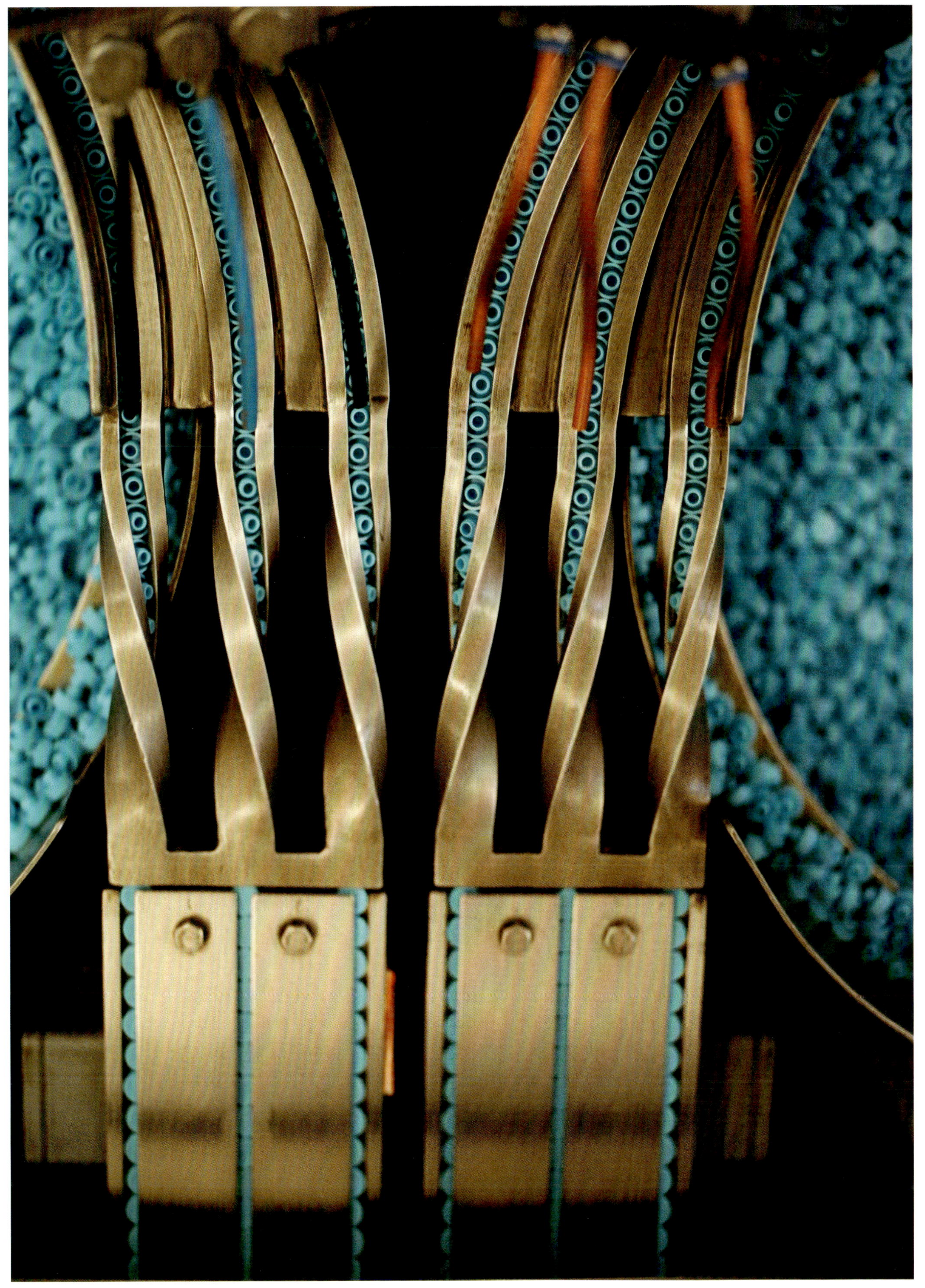

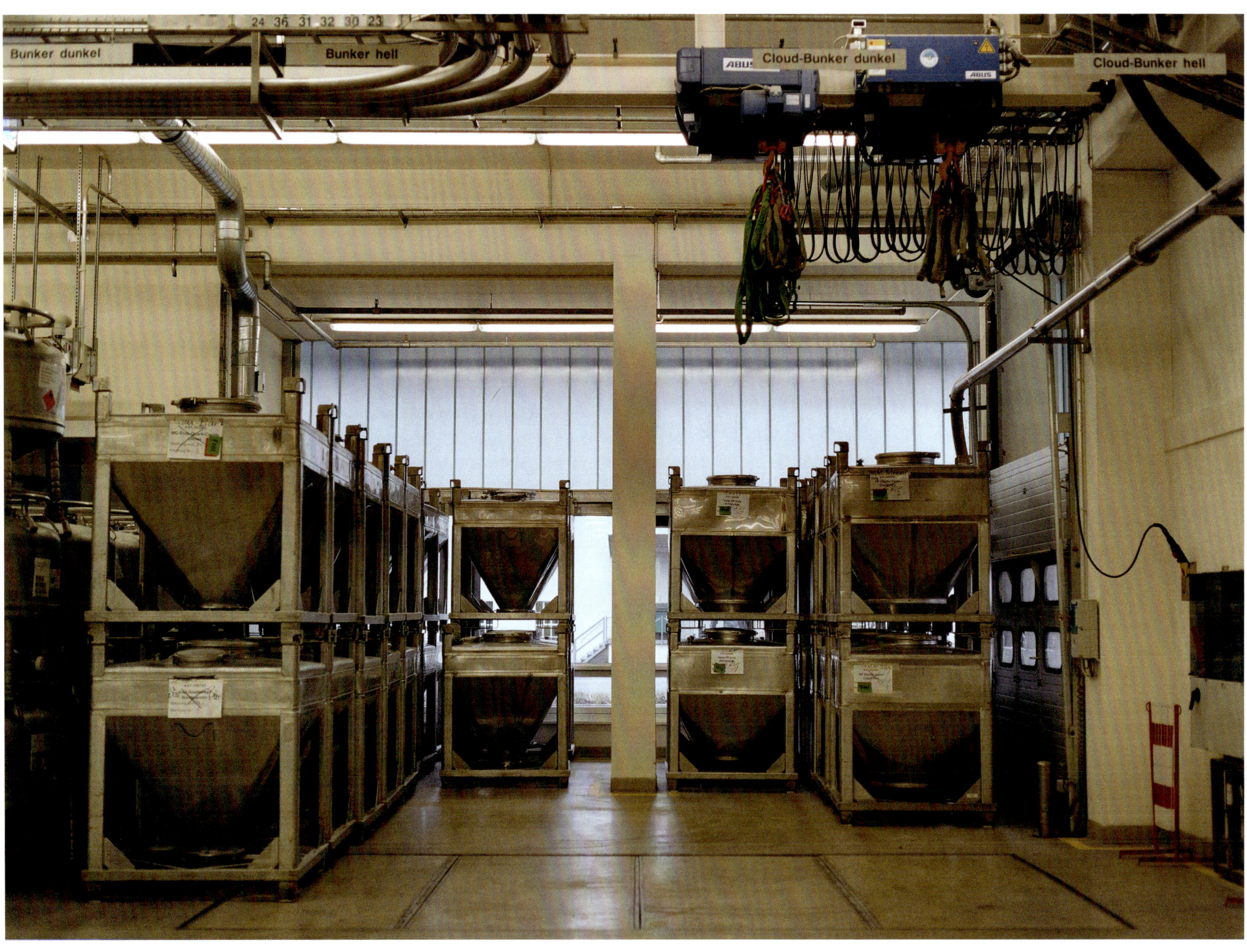
24 36 31 32 30 23
Bunker dunkel
Bunker hell
ABUS
Cloud-Bunker dunkel
ABUS
Cloud-Bunker hell

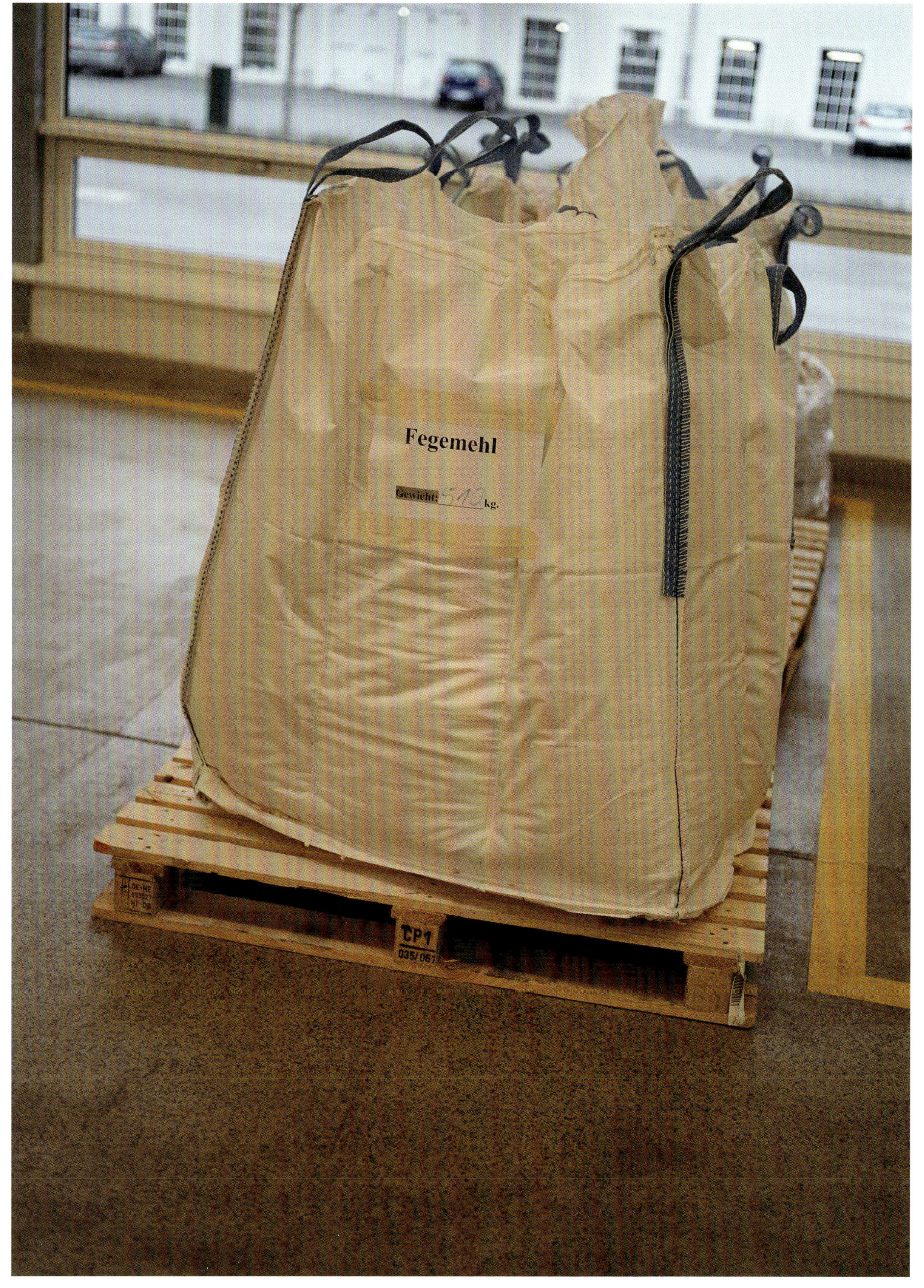

Fegemehl
Gewicht: 510 kg.

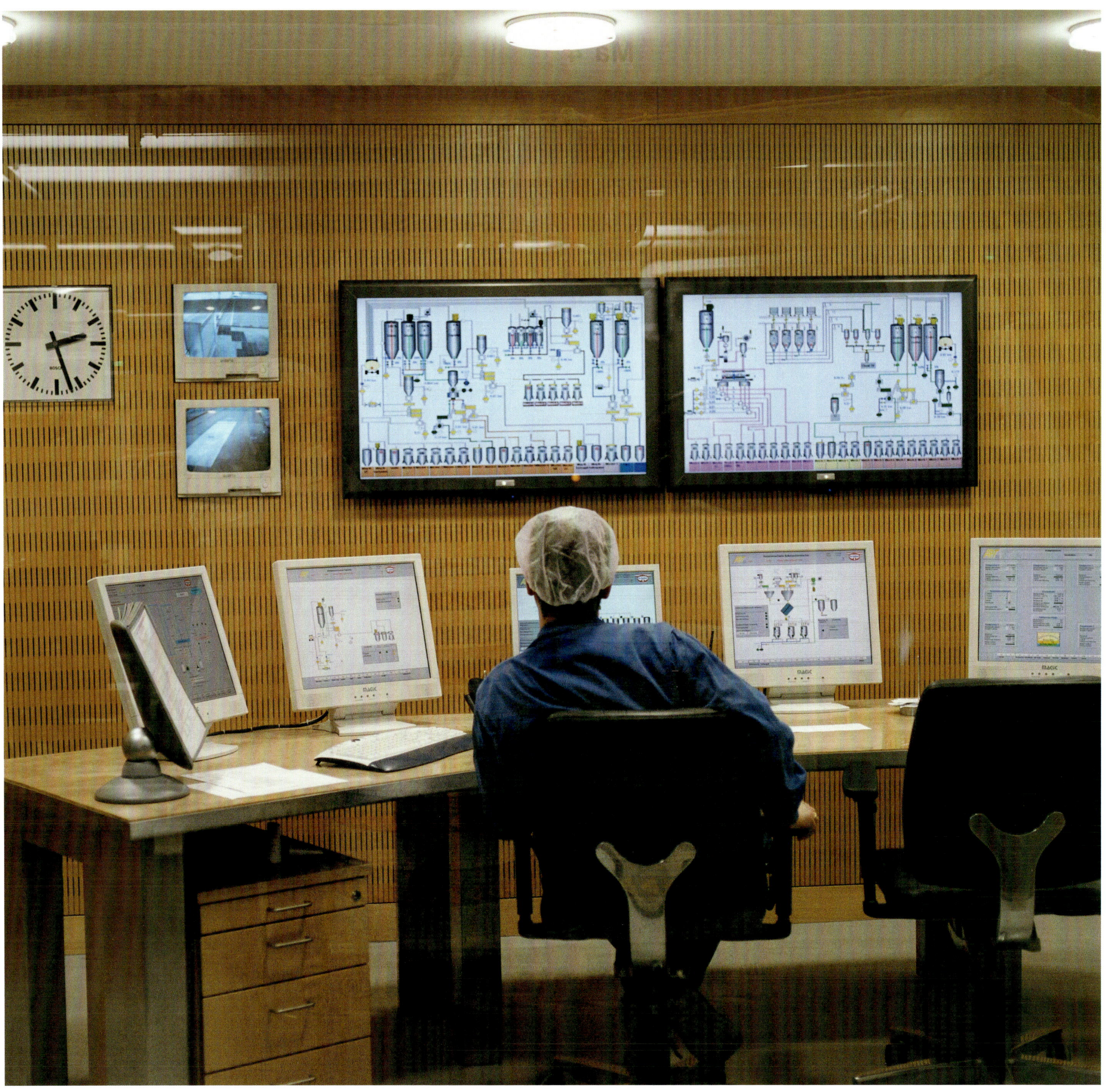

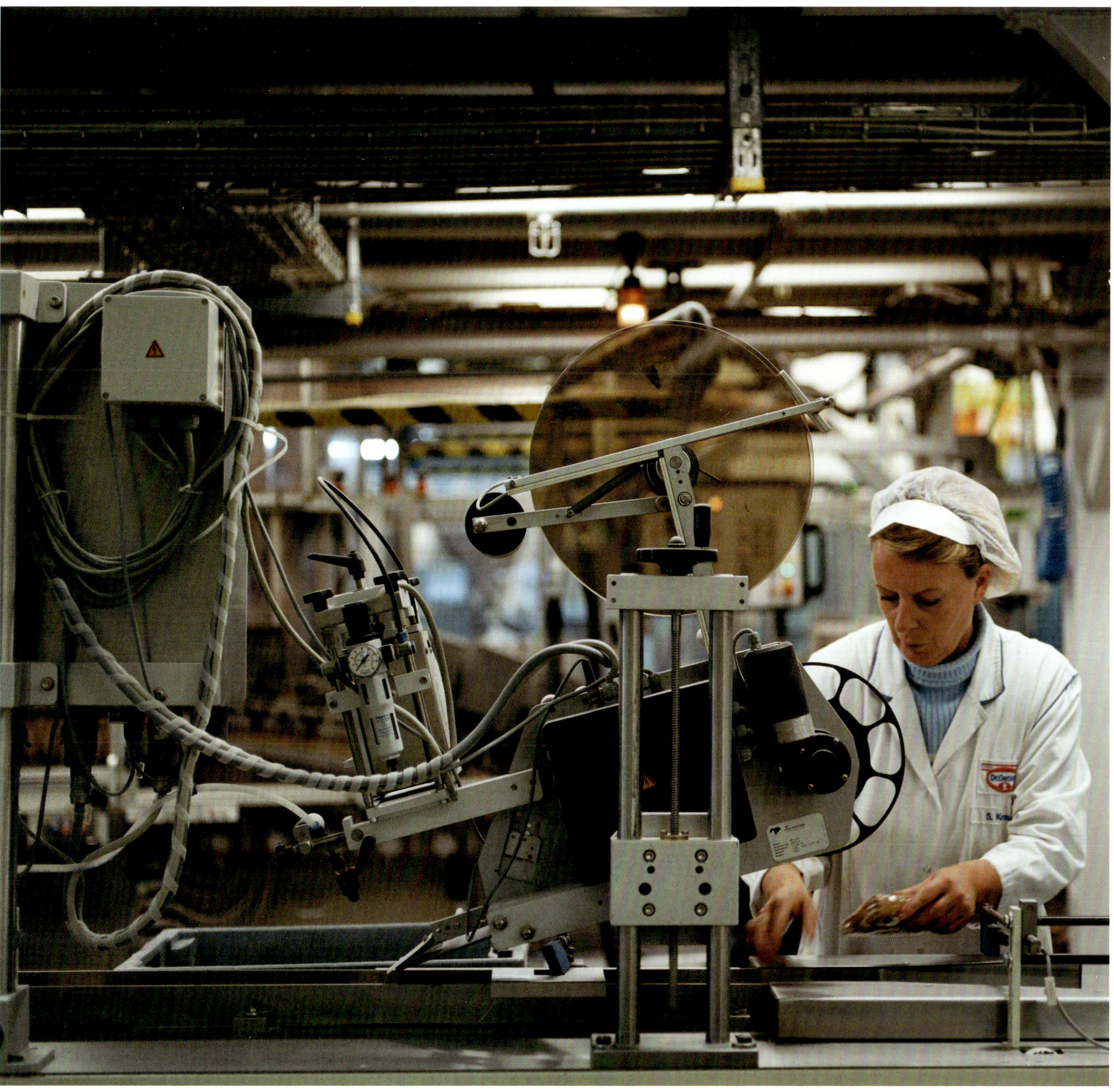

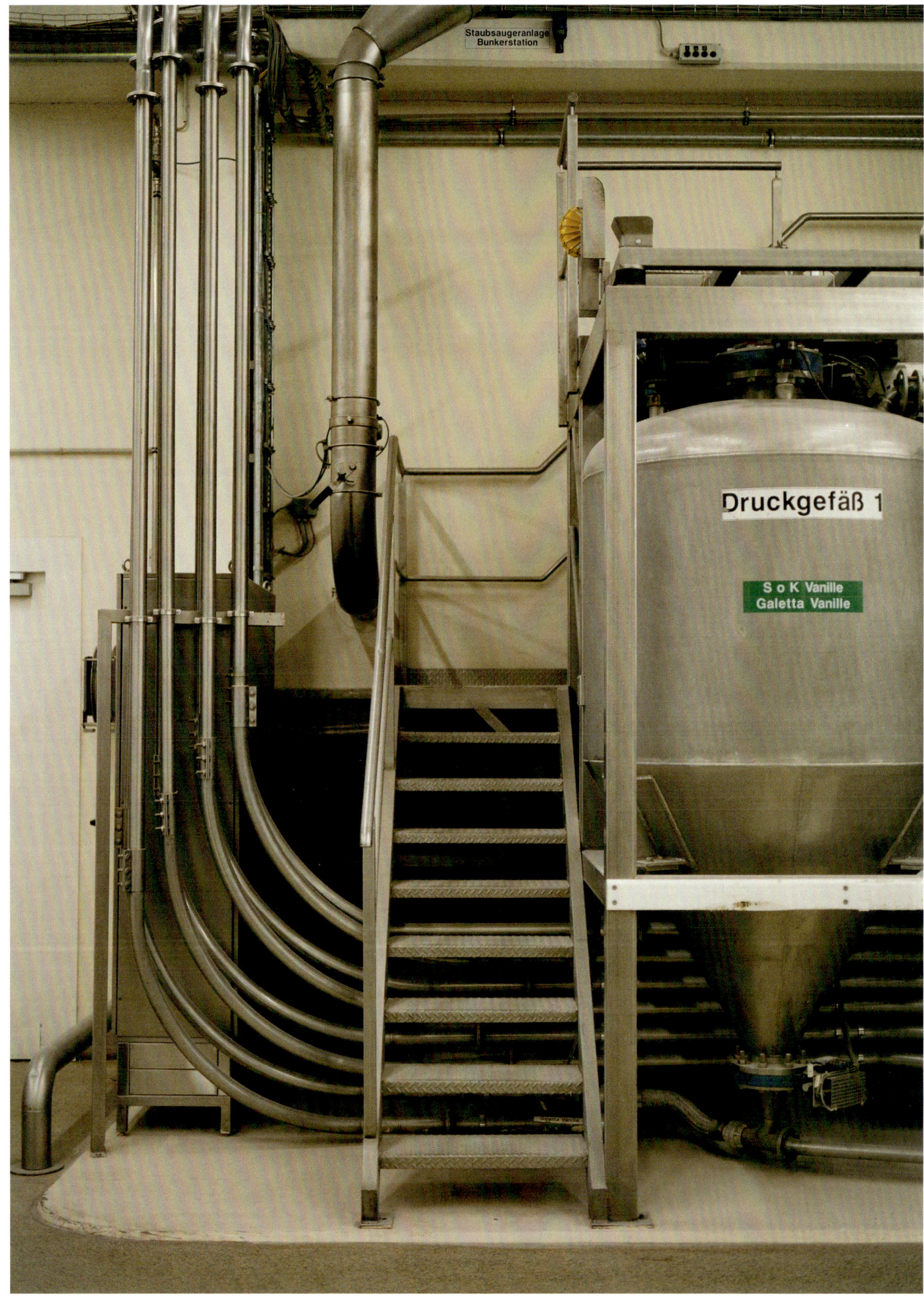

Staubsaugeranlage
Bunkerstation
Druckgefäß 1
S o K Vanille
Galetta Vanille

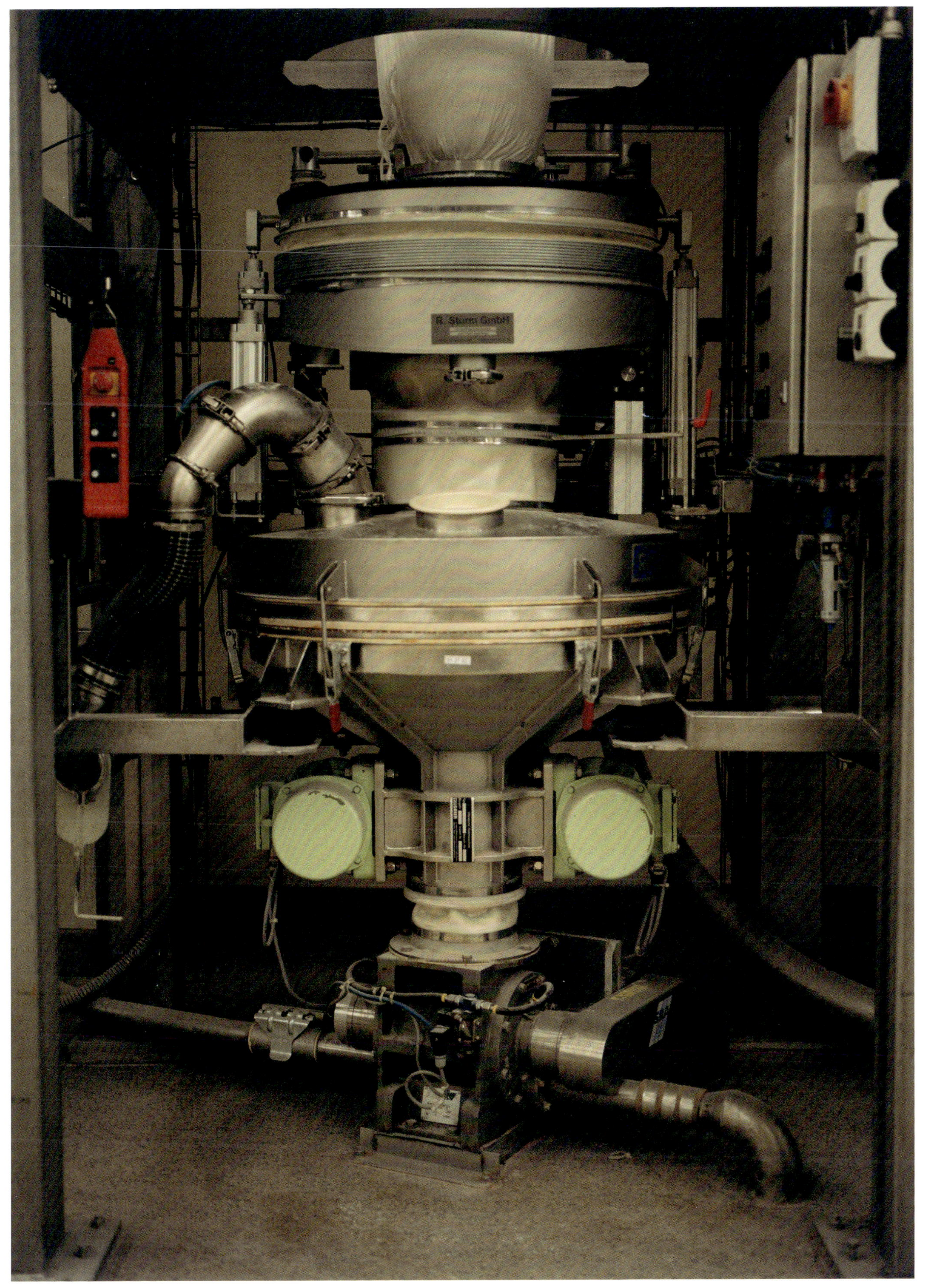

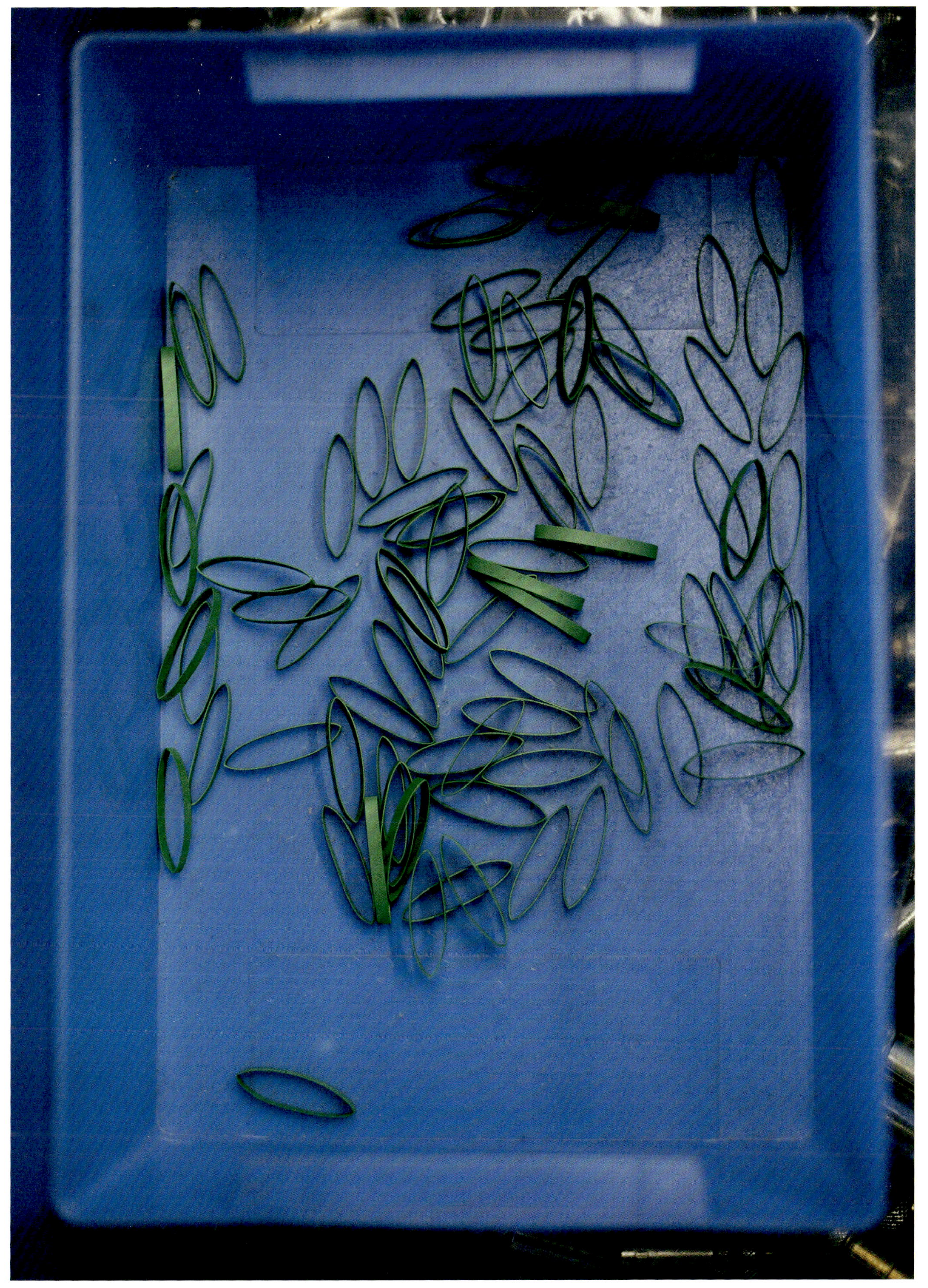

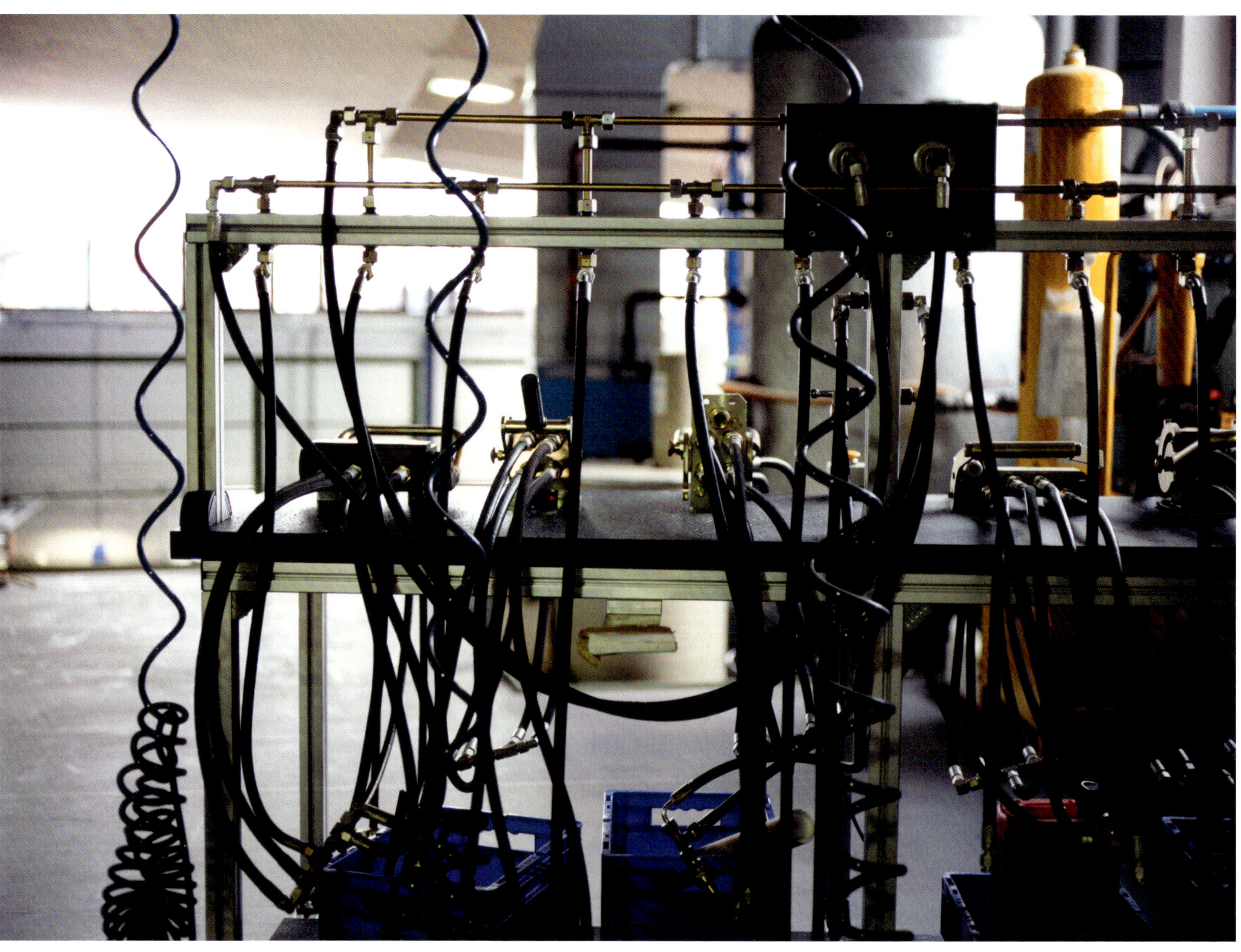

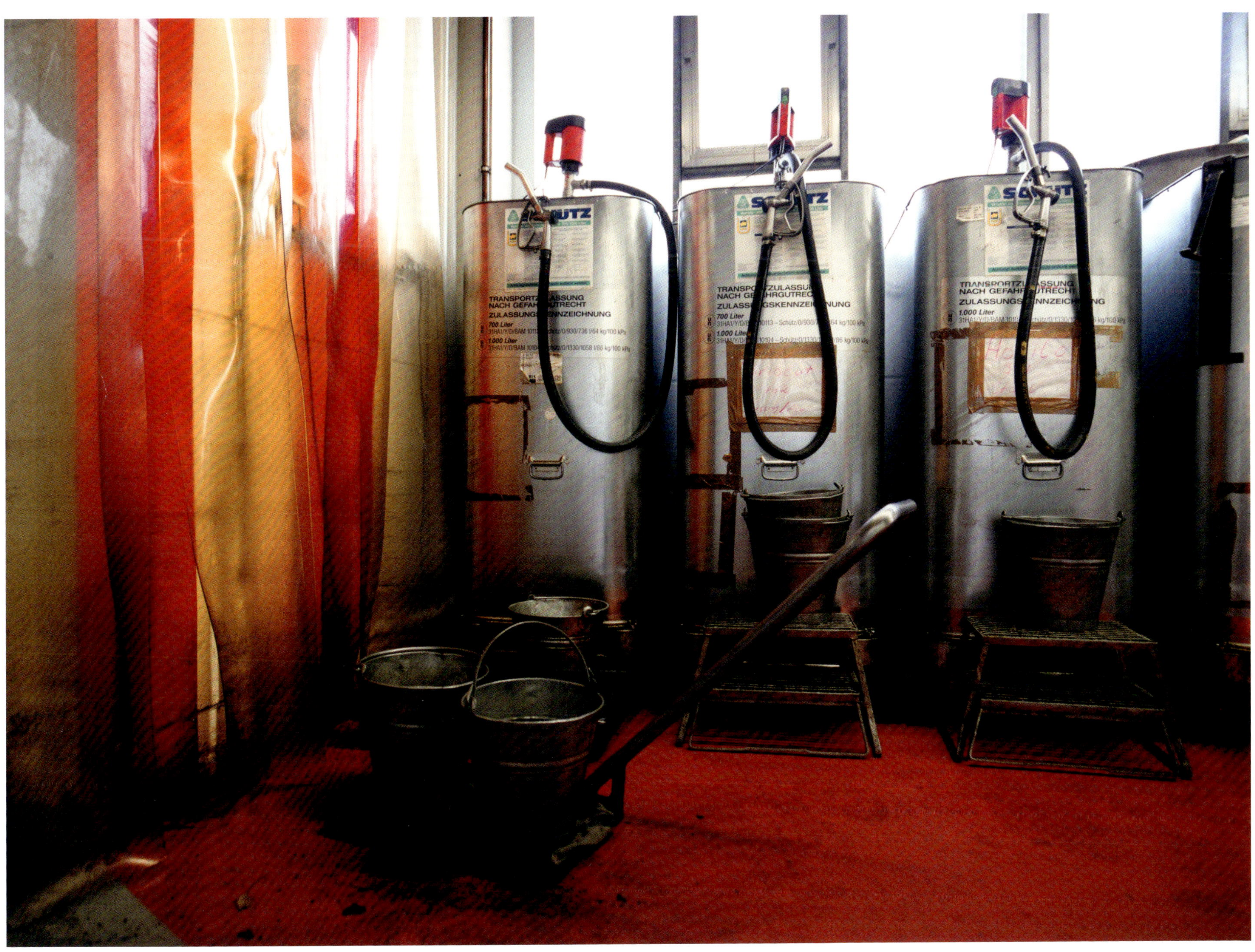

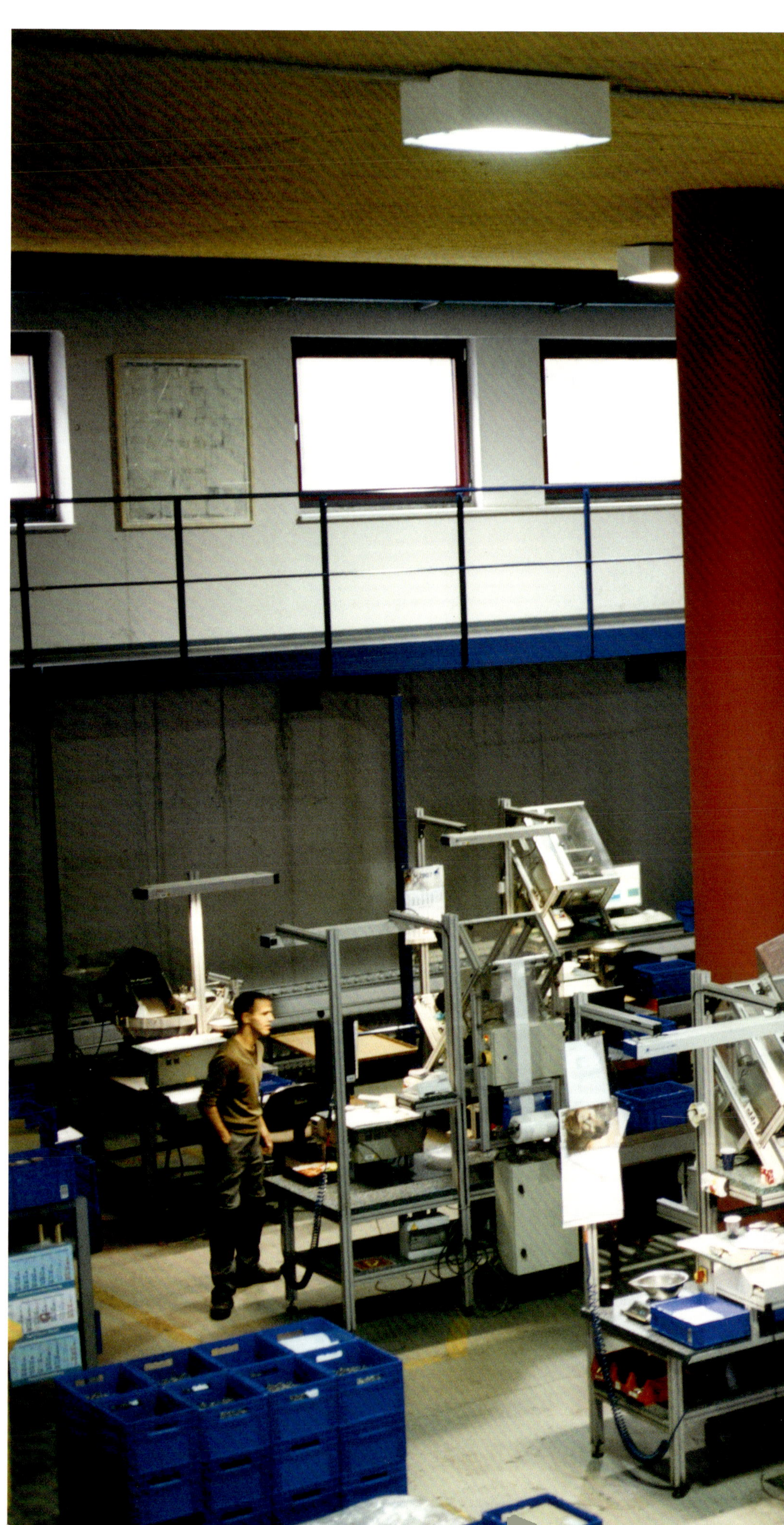

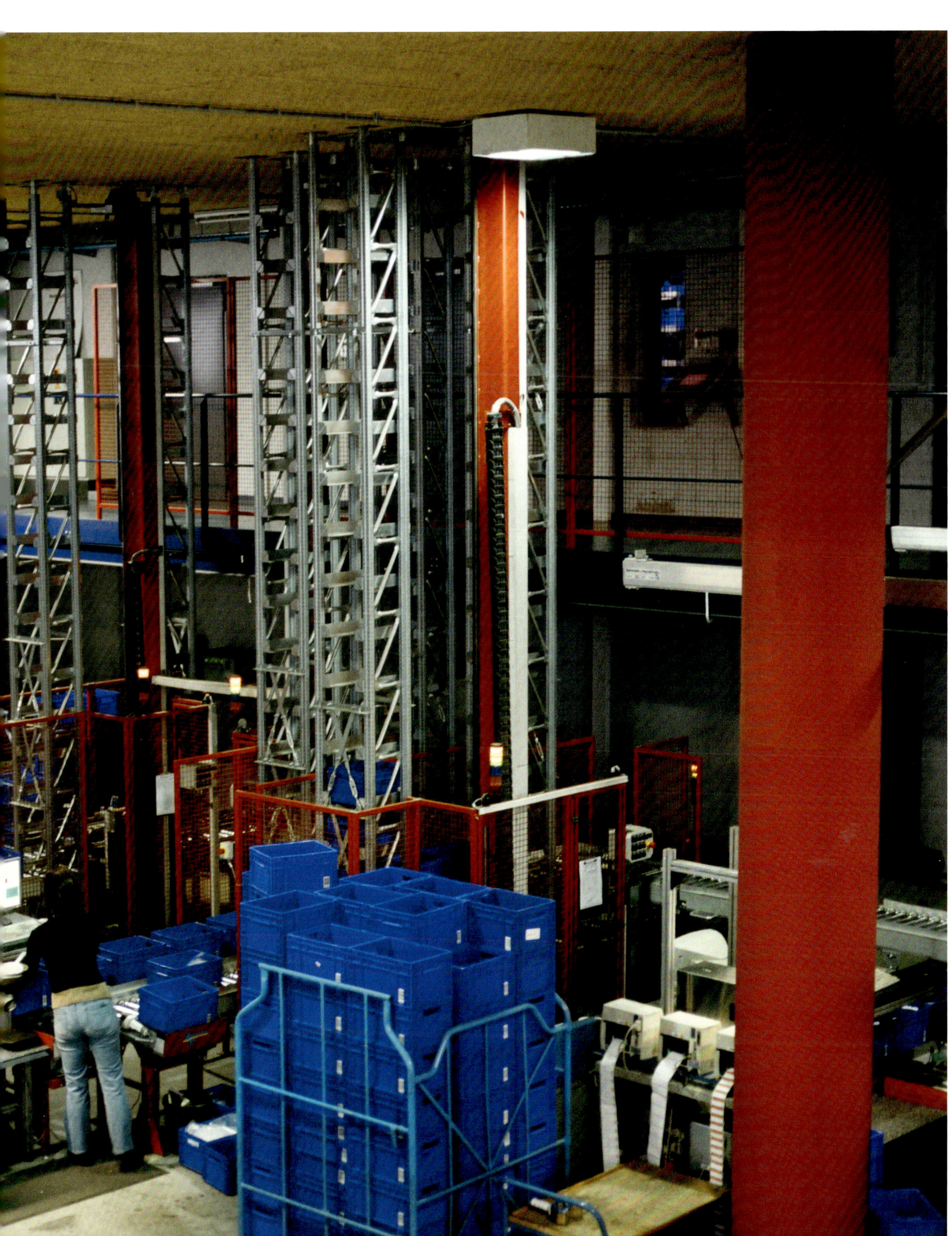

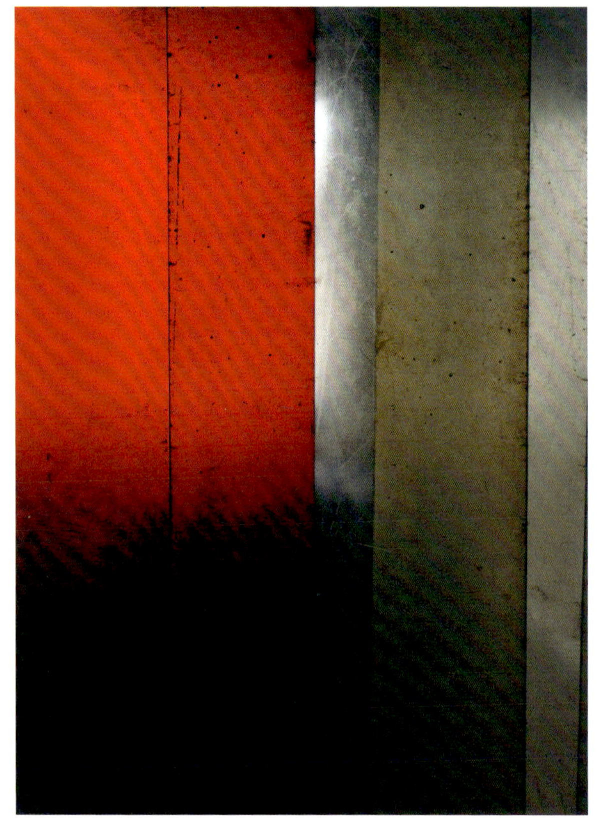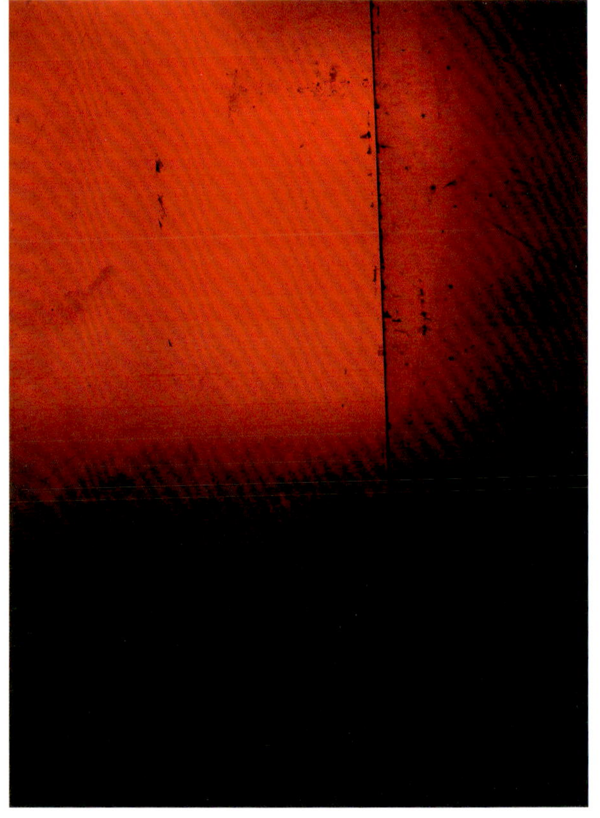

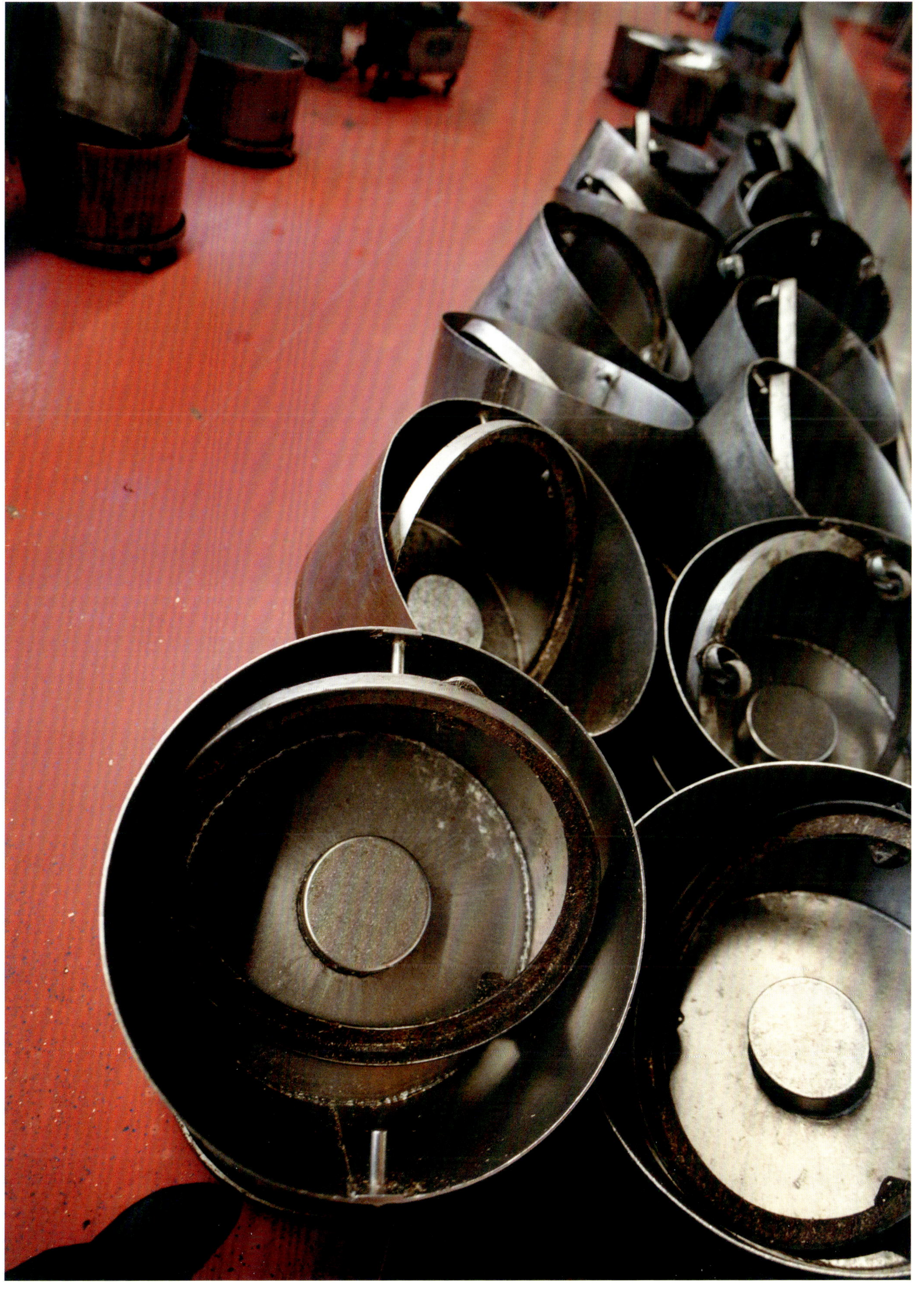

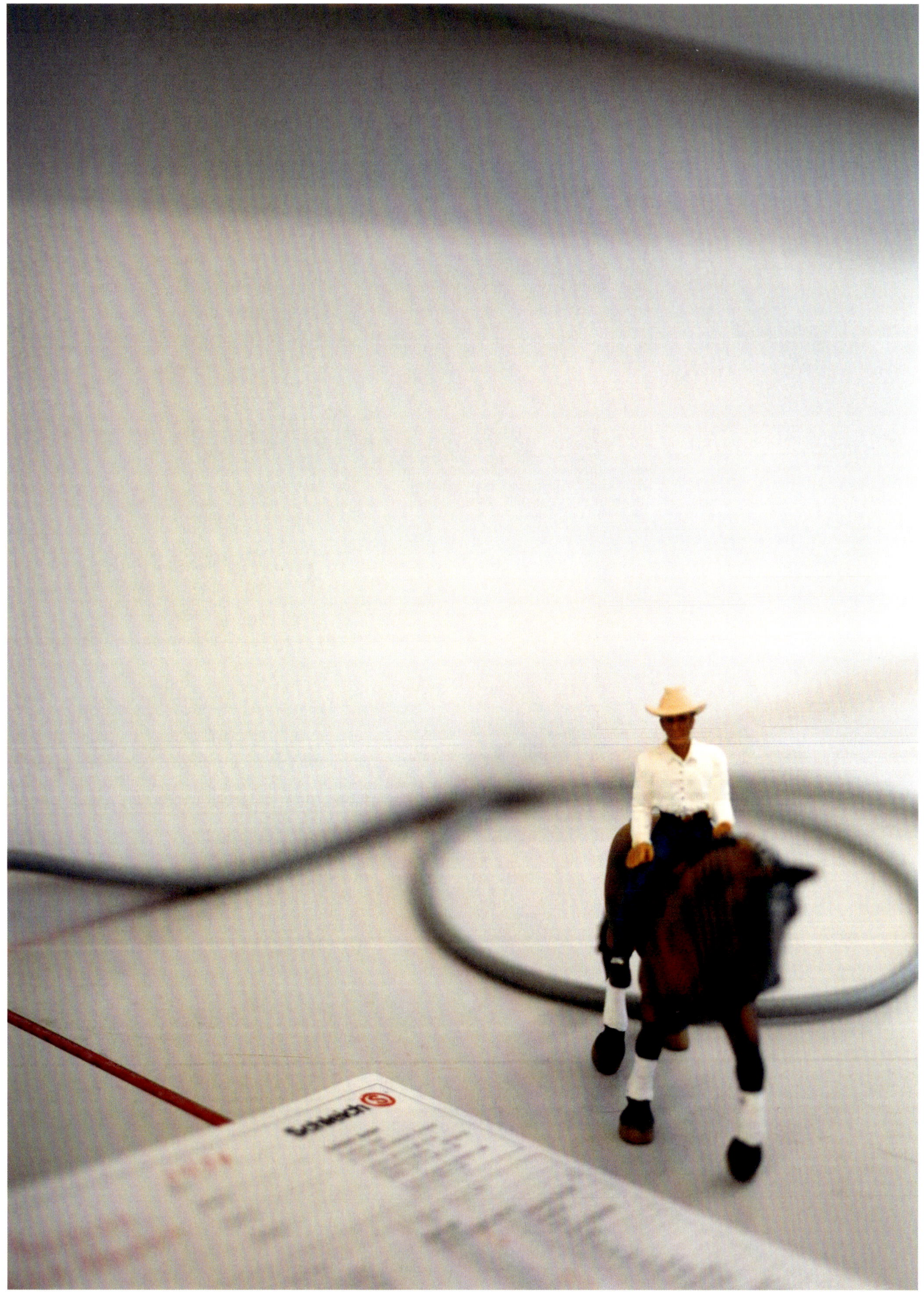

　Schleich

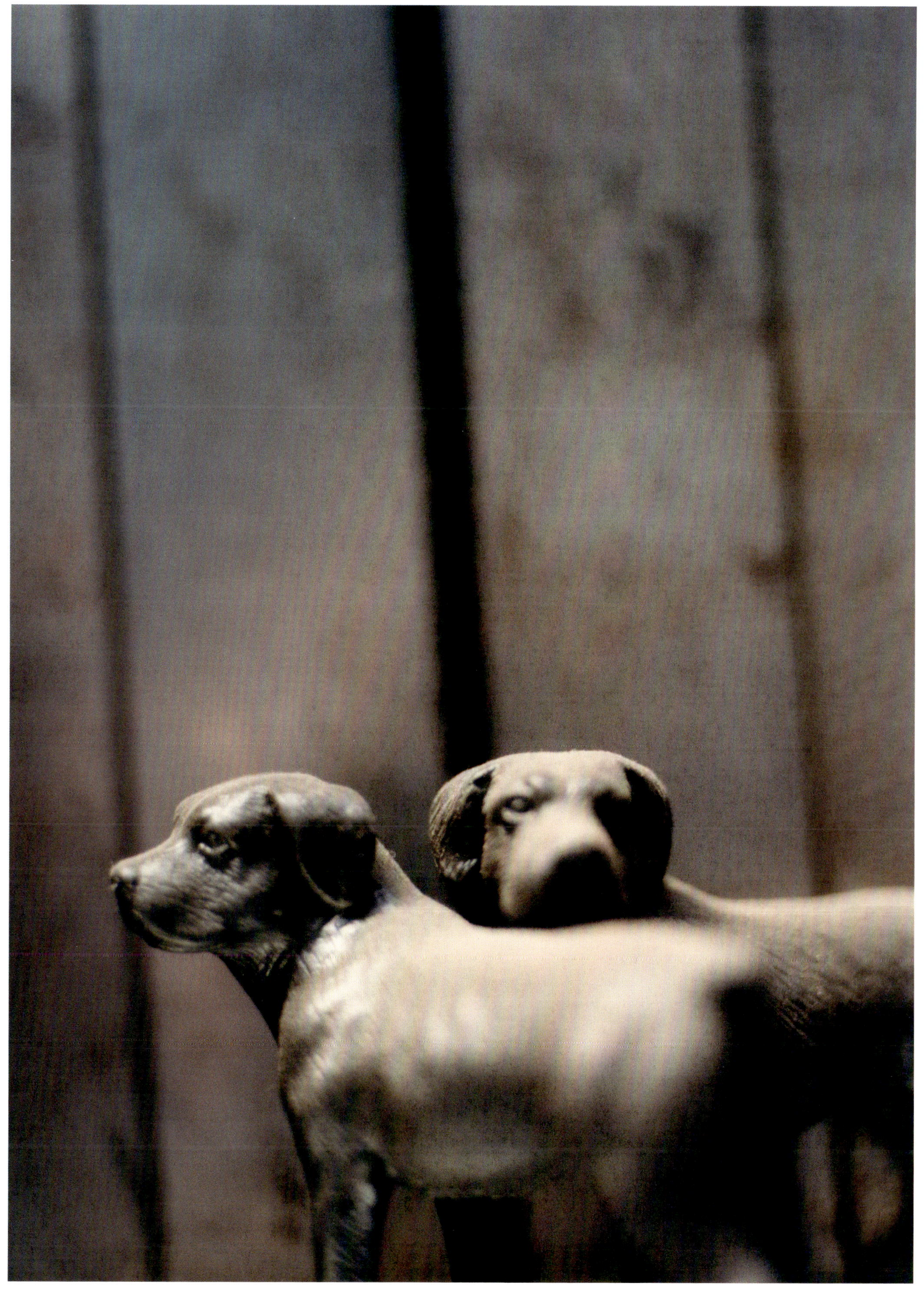

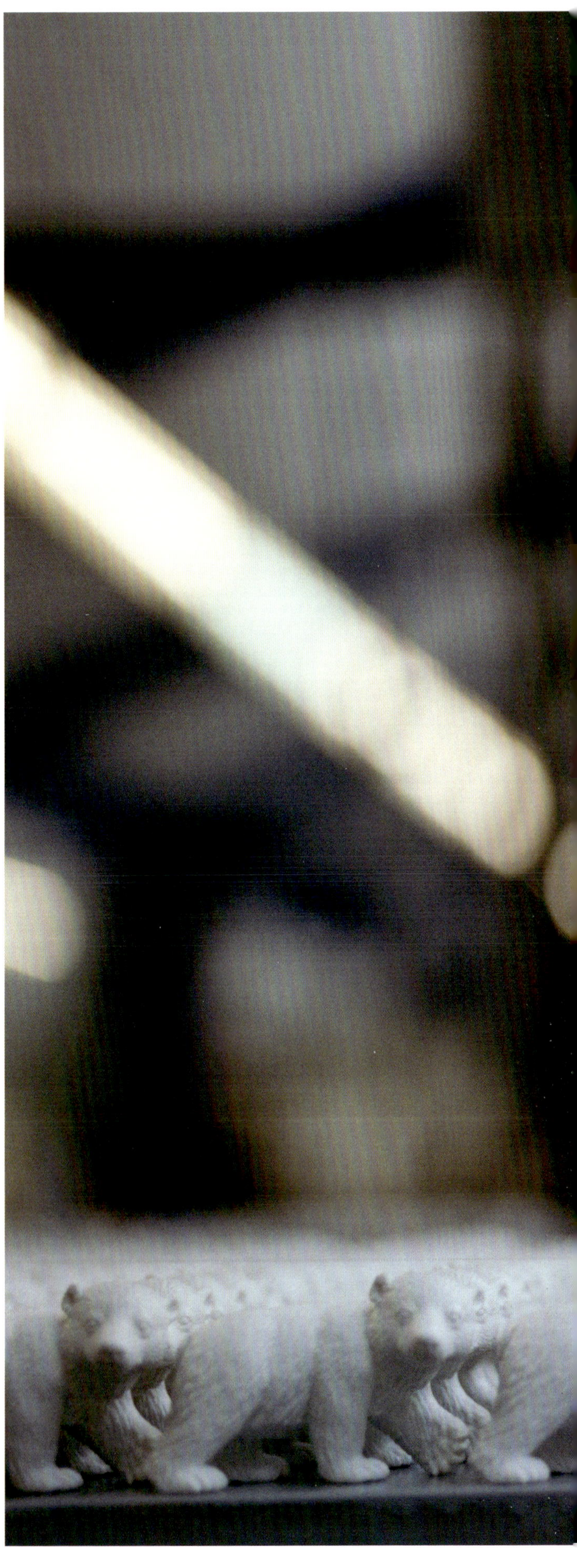

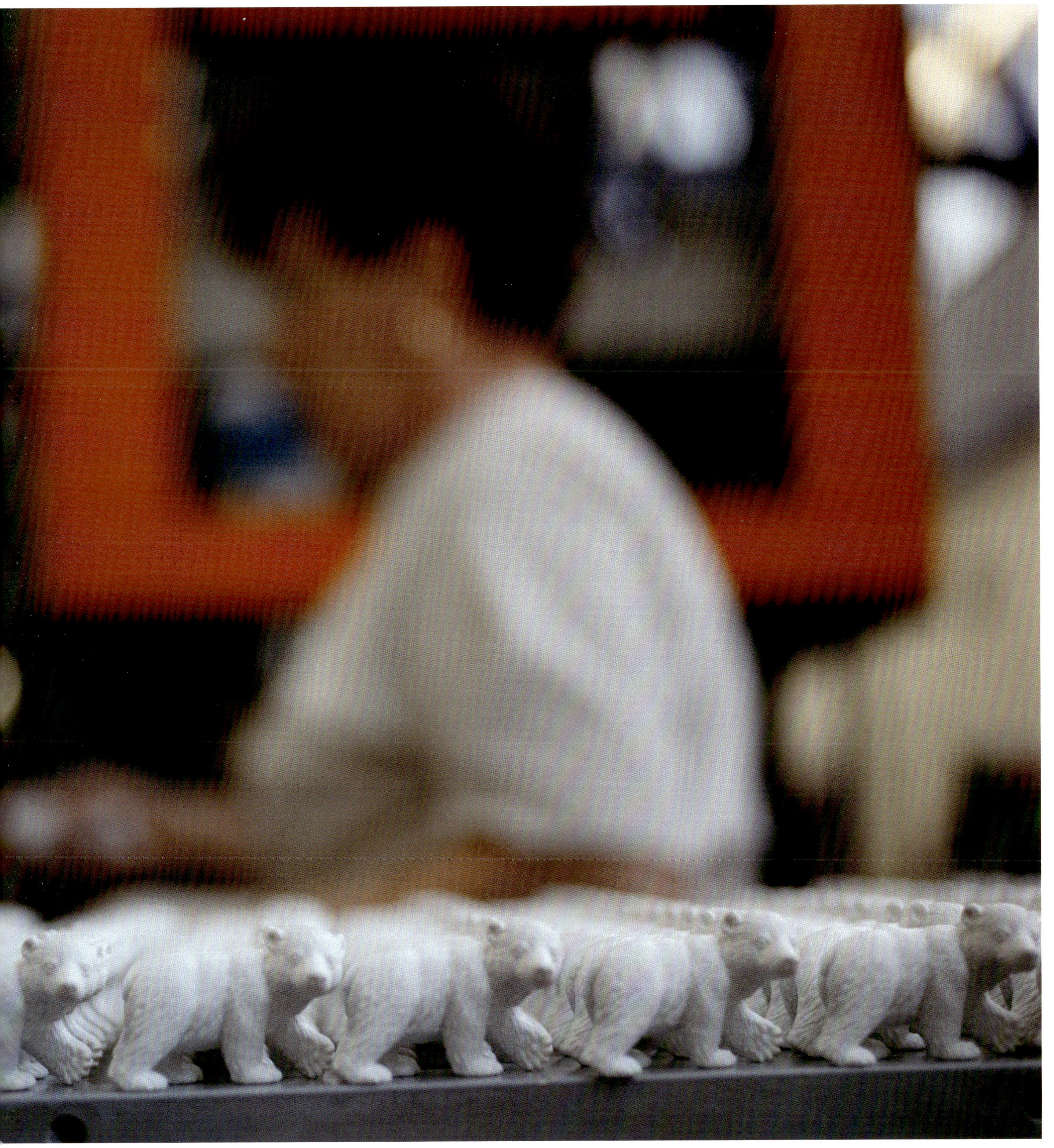

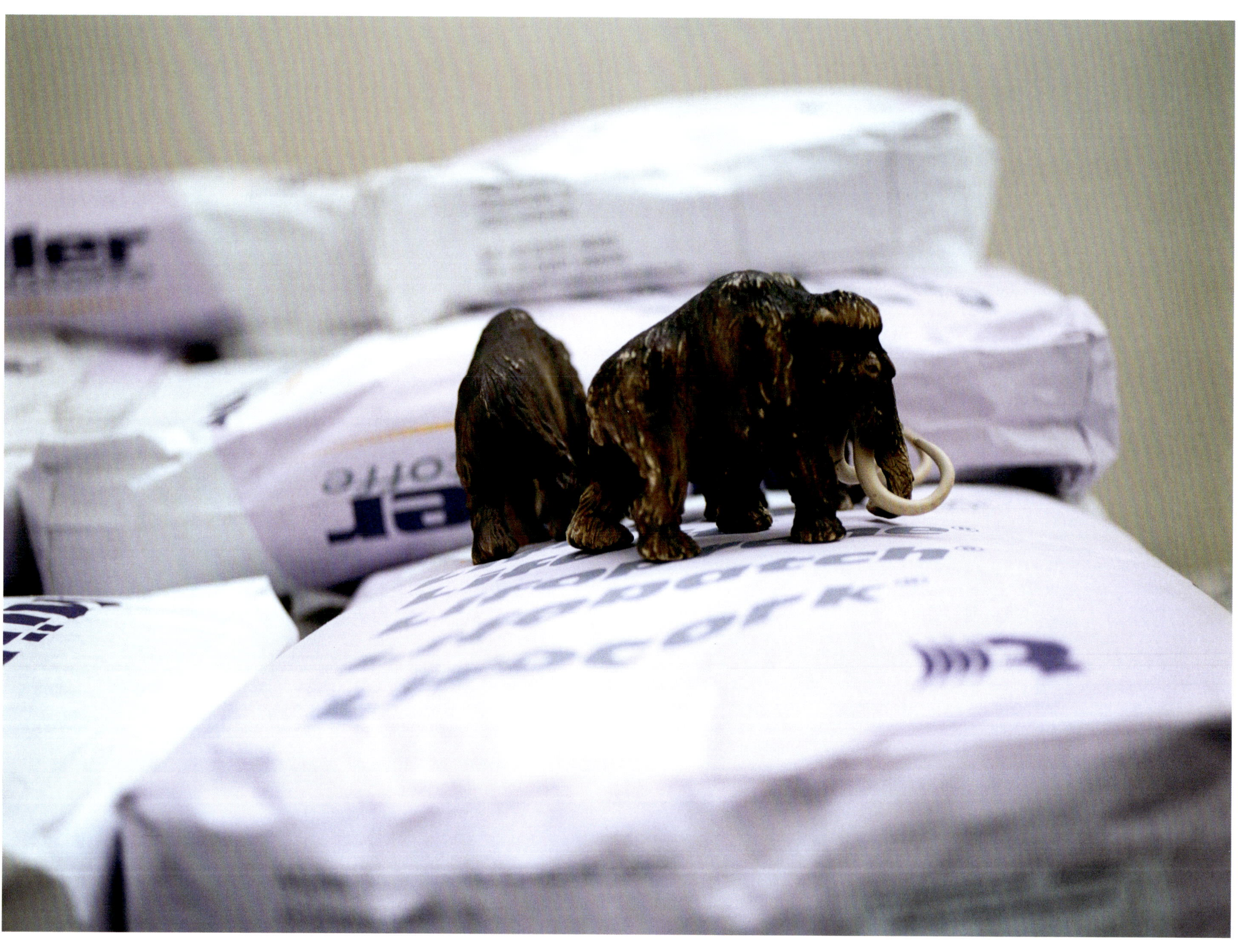

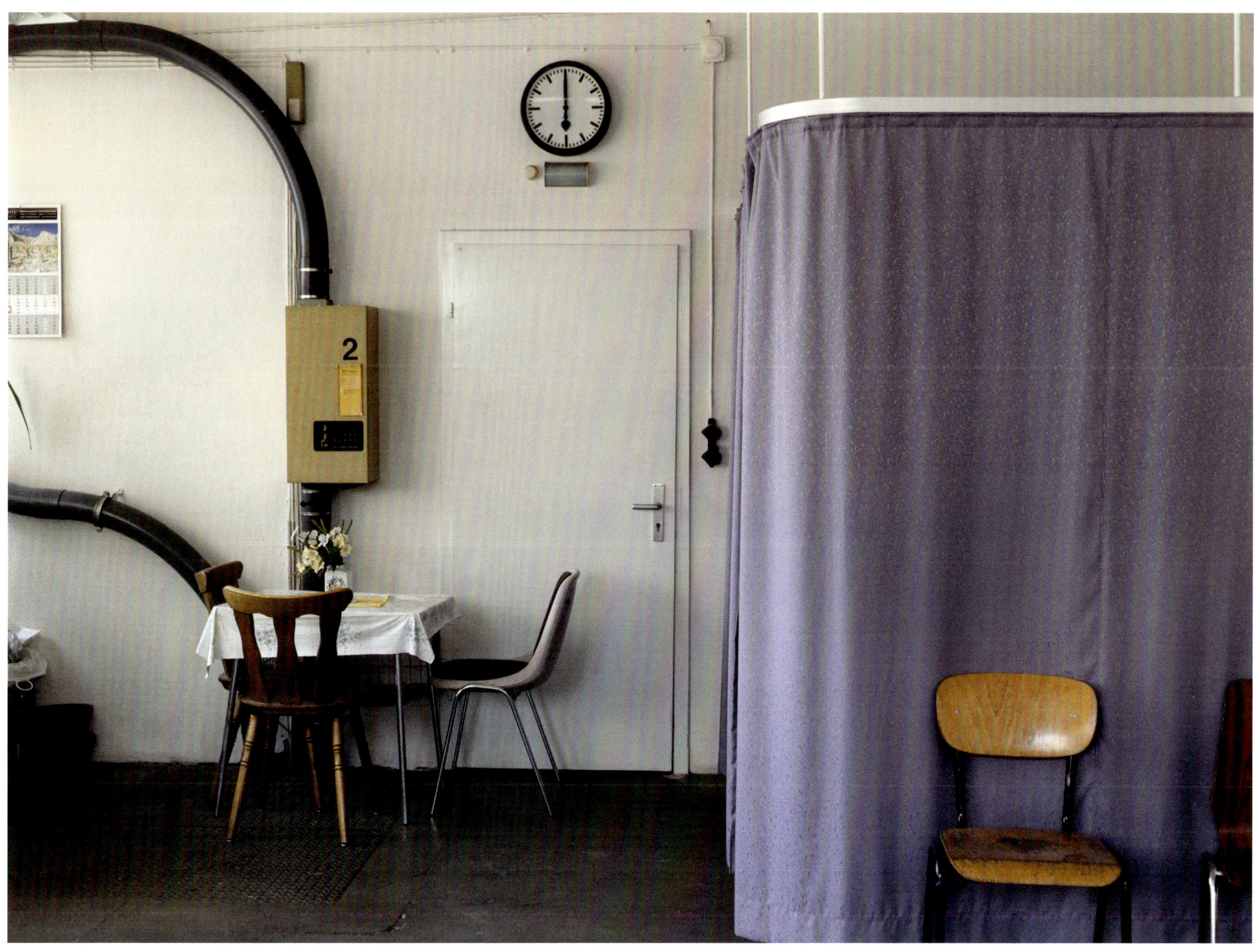

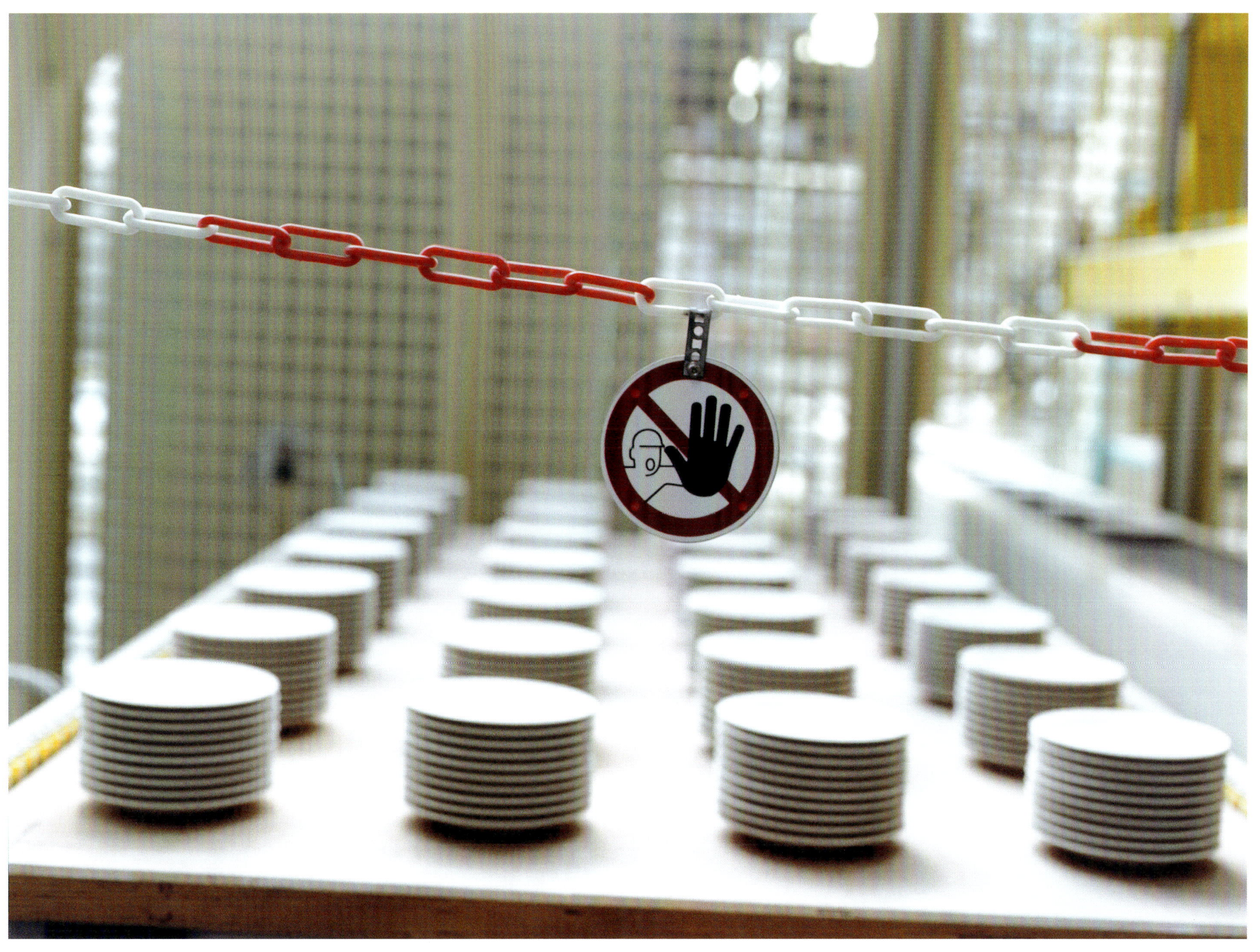

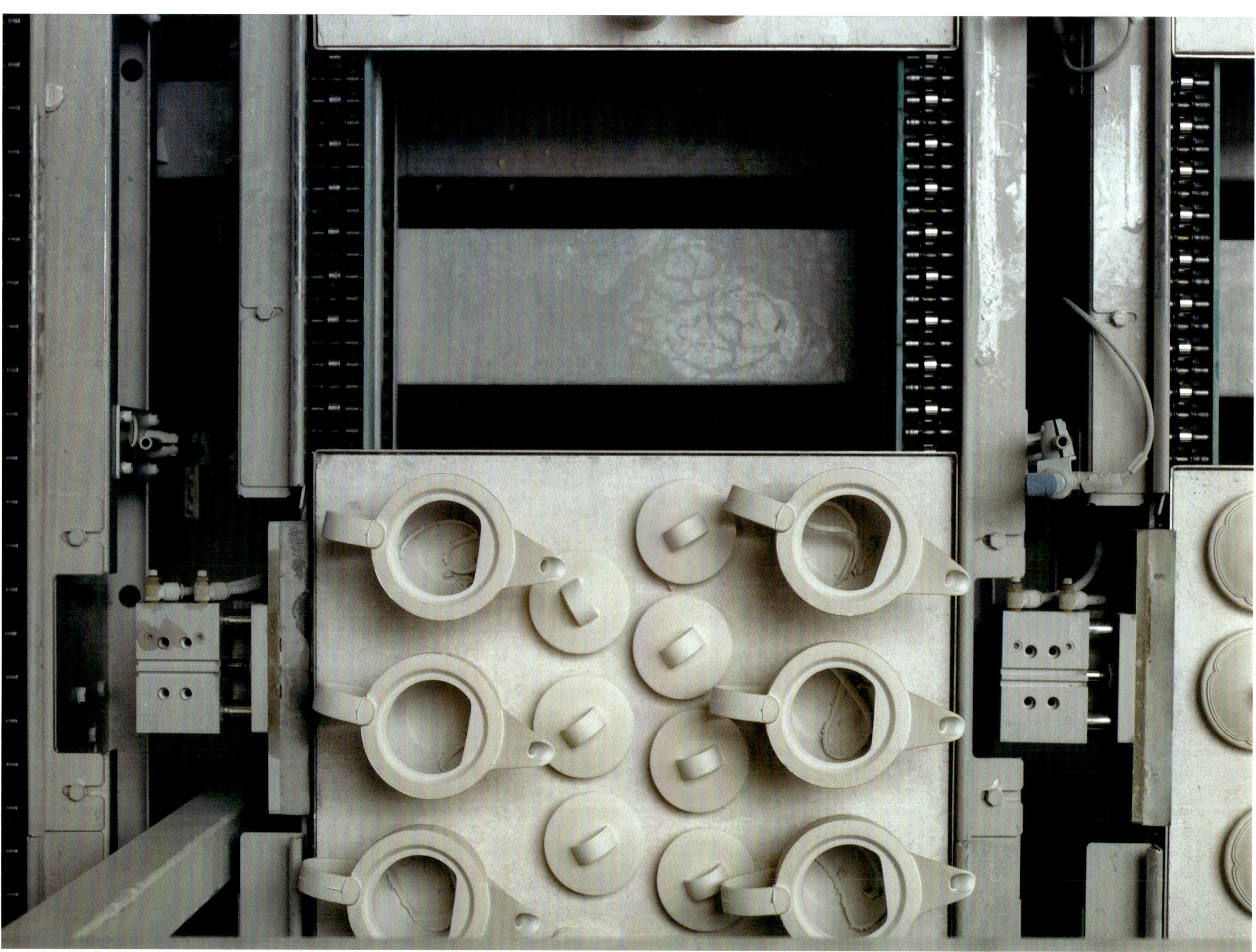

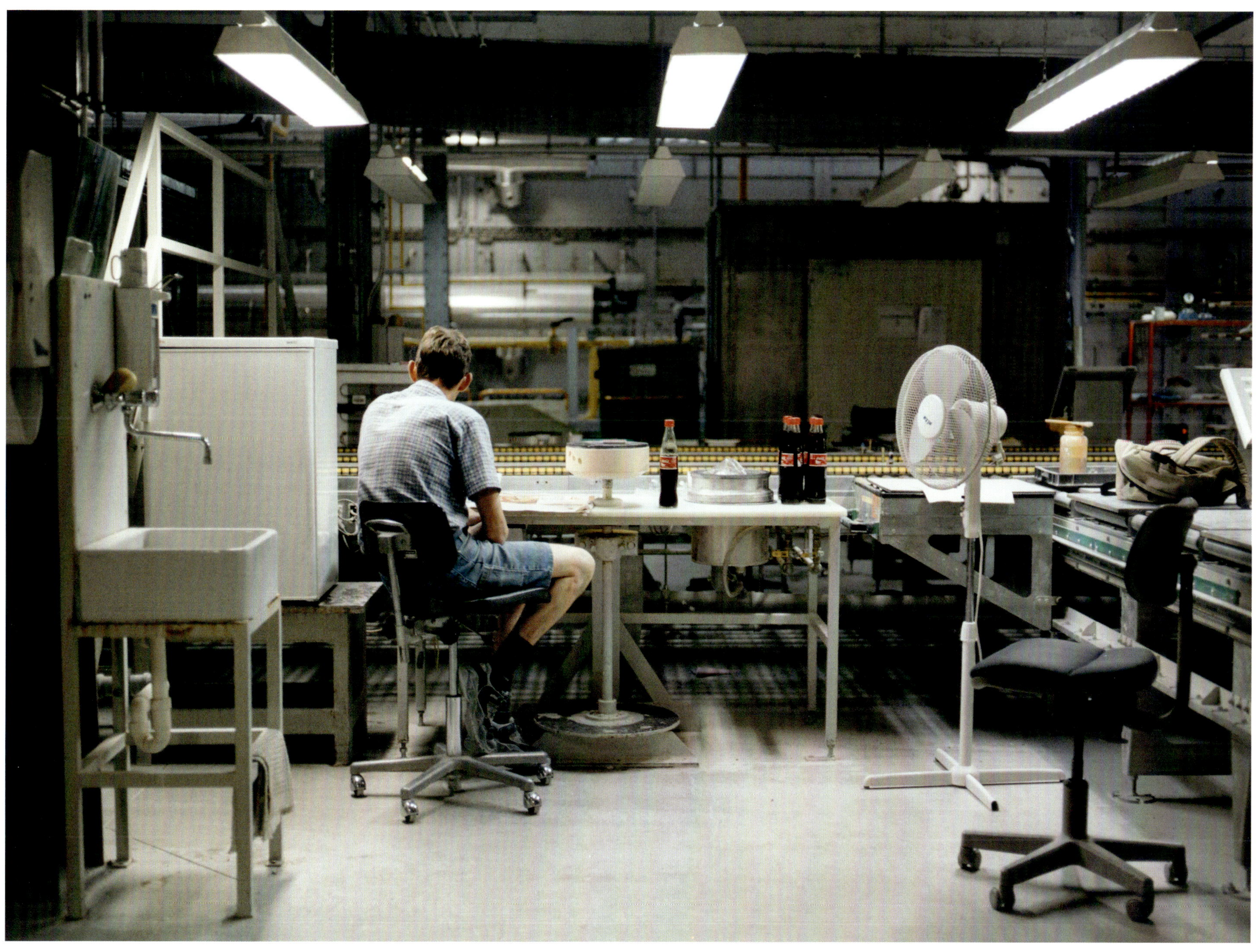

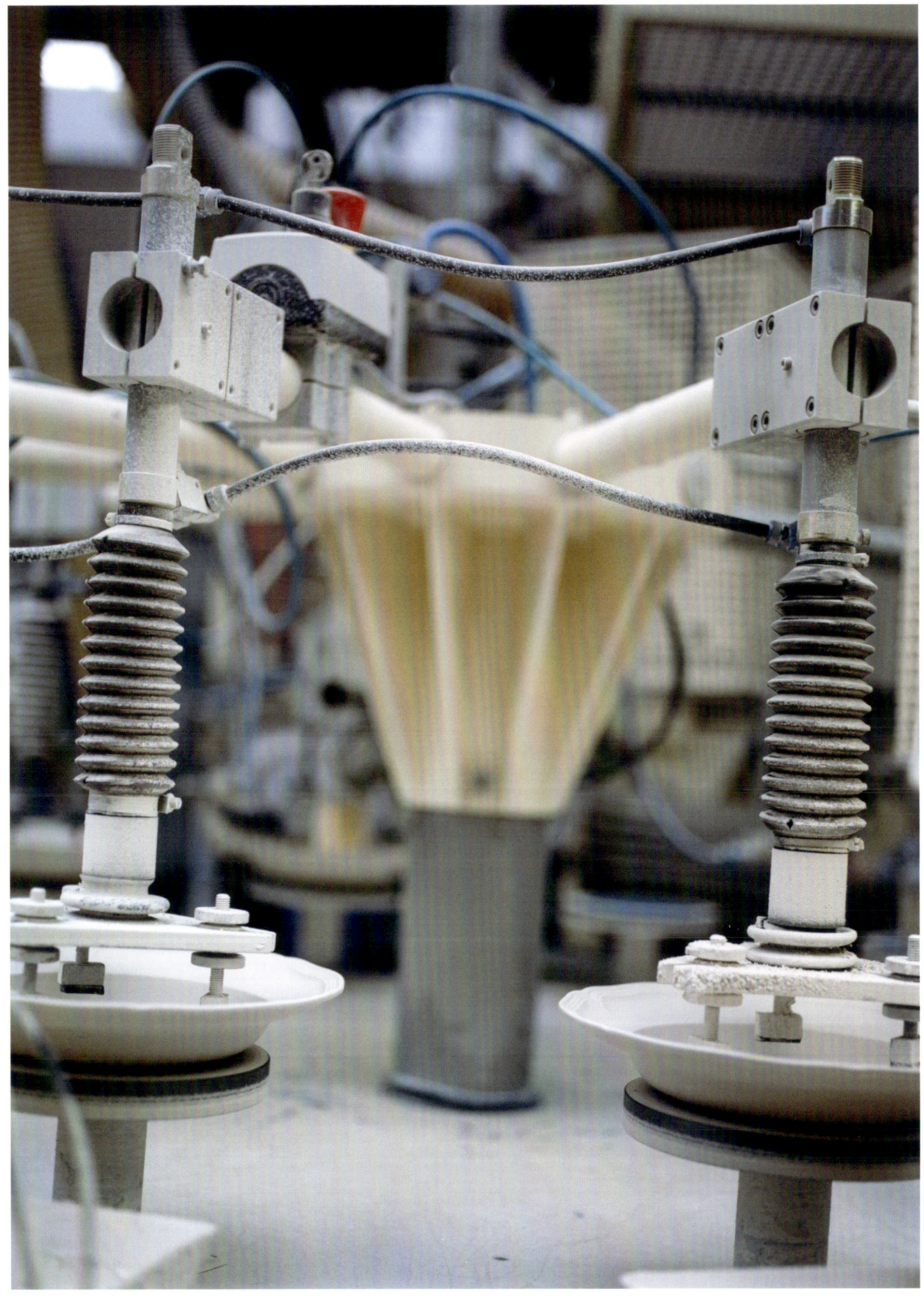

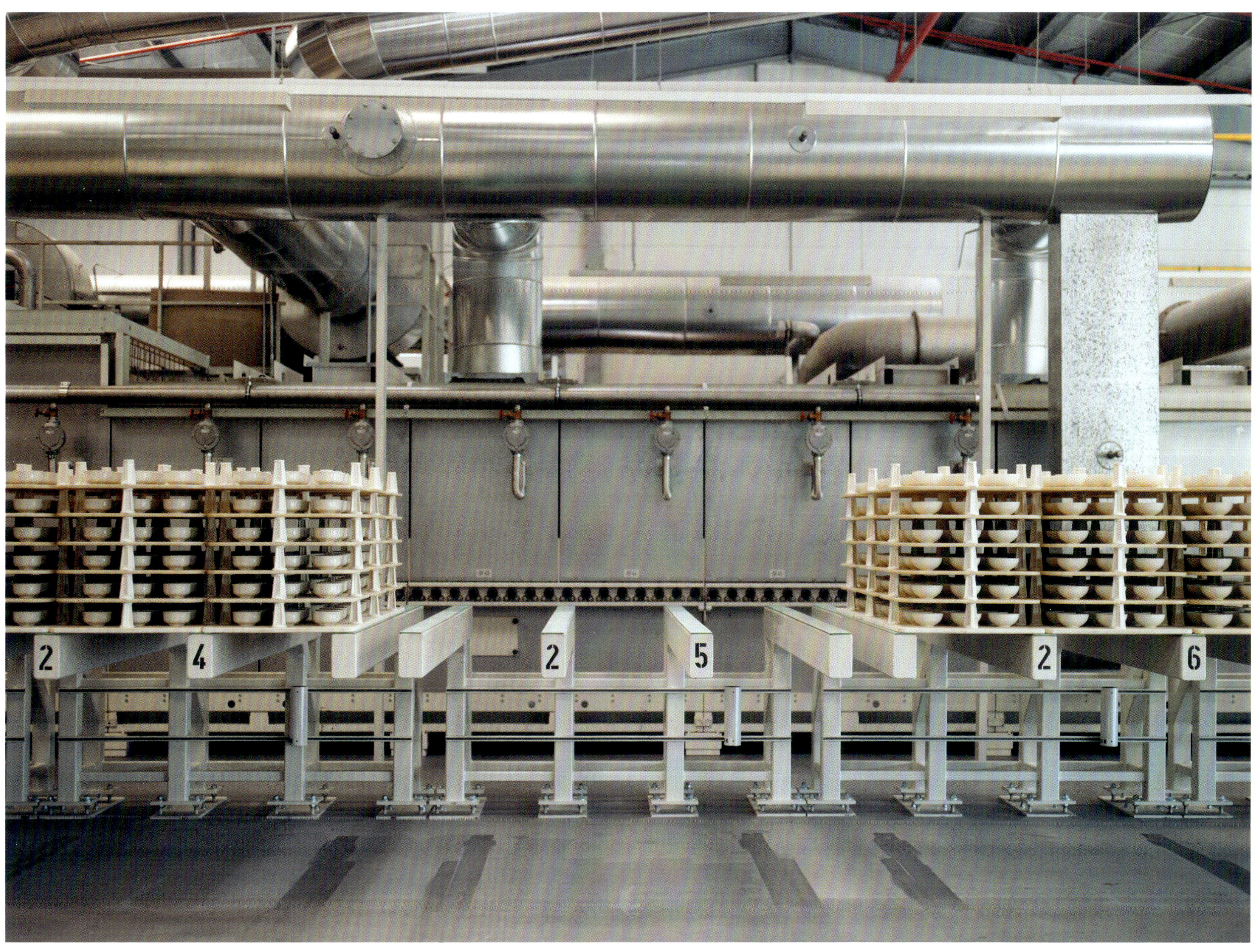

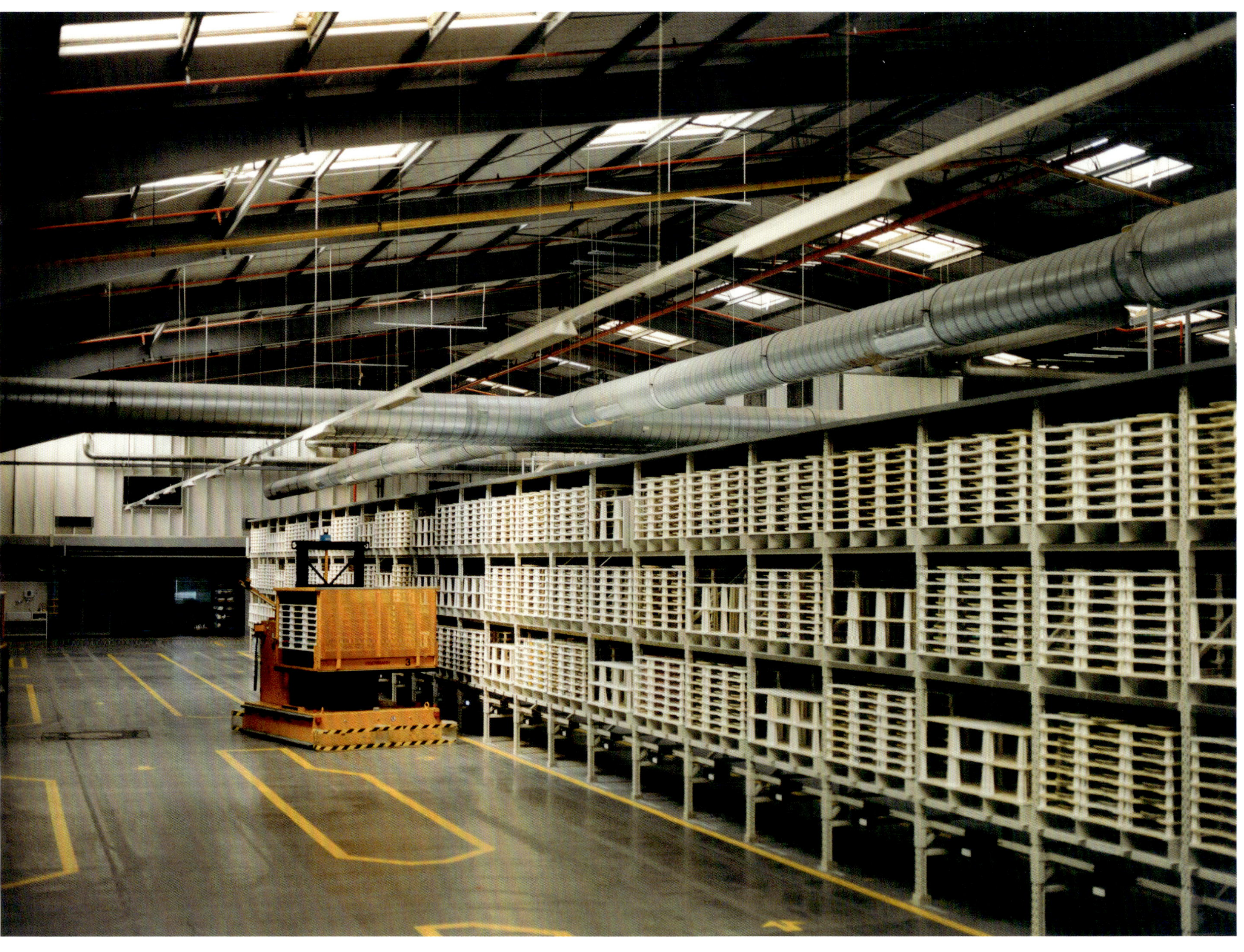

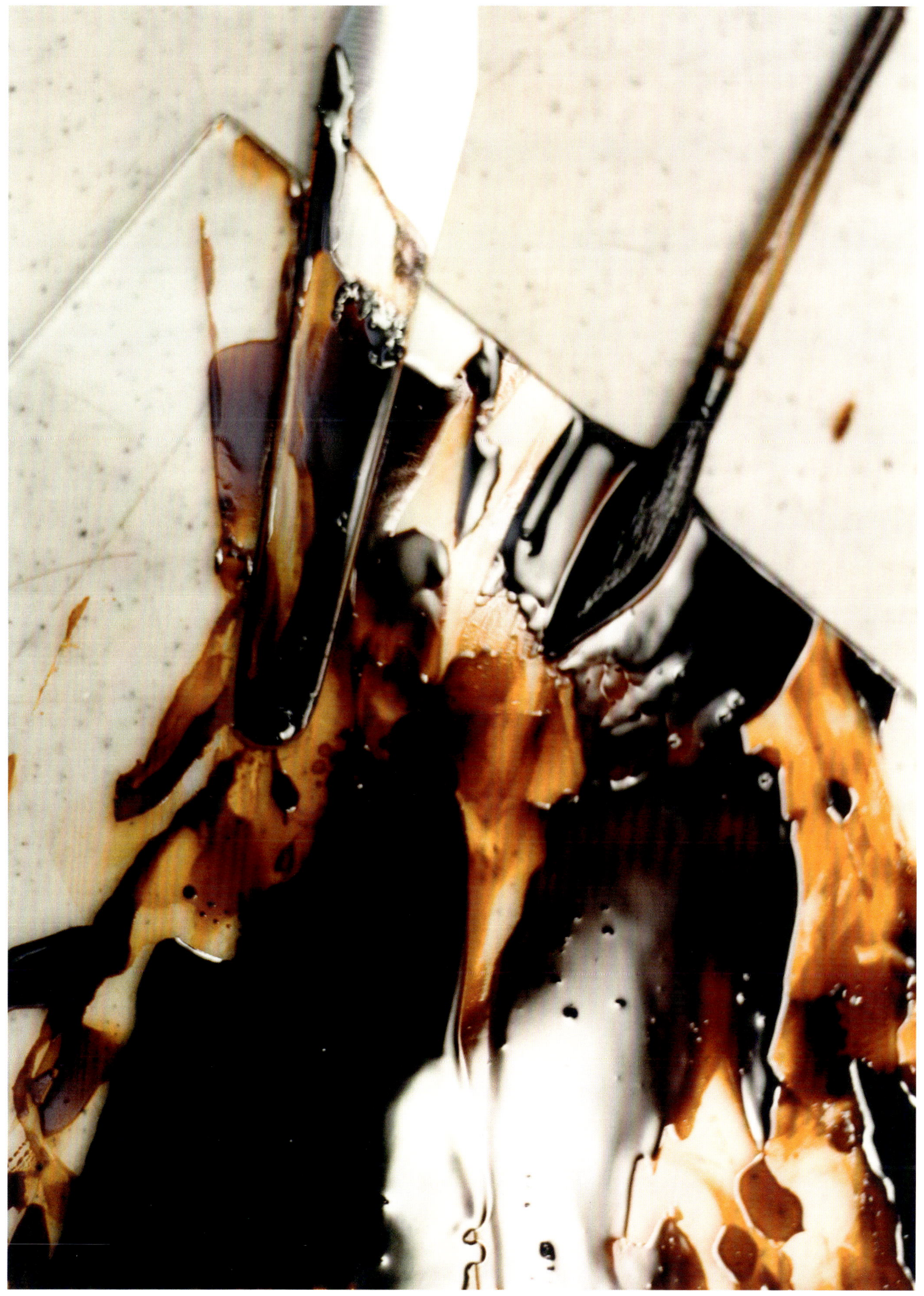

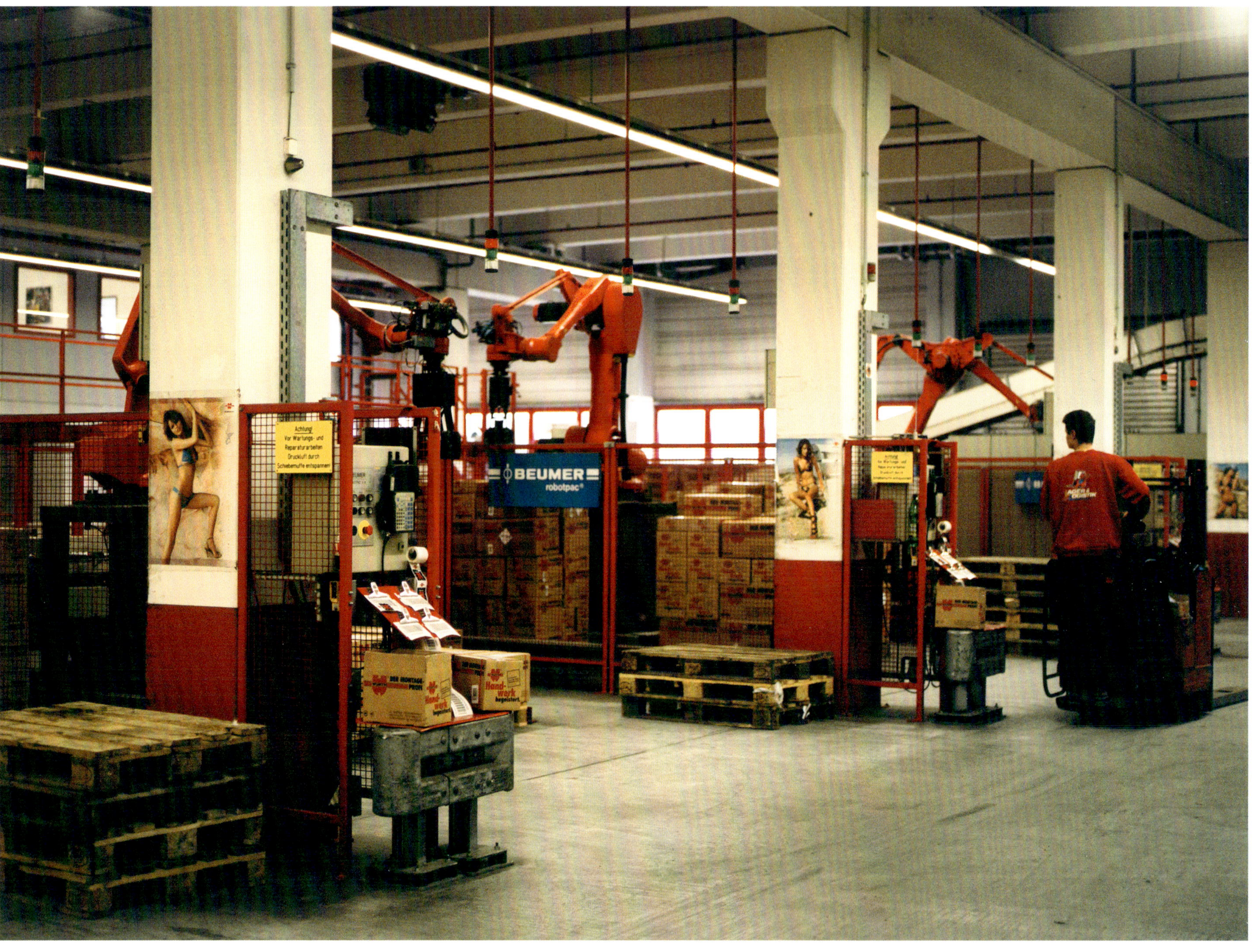

BEUMER
robotpac®
Achtung
Vor Wartungs- und
Reparaturarbeiten
Druckluft durch
Schiebemuffe entspannen
Hand-
werk
begeistert

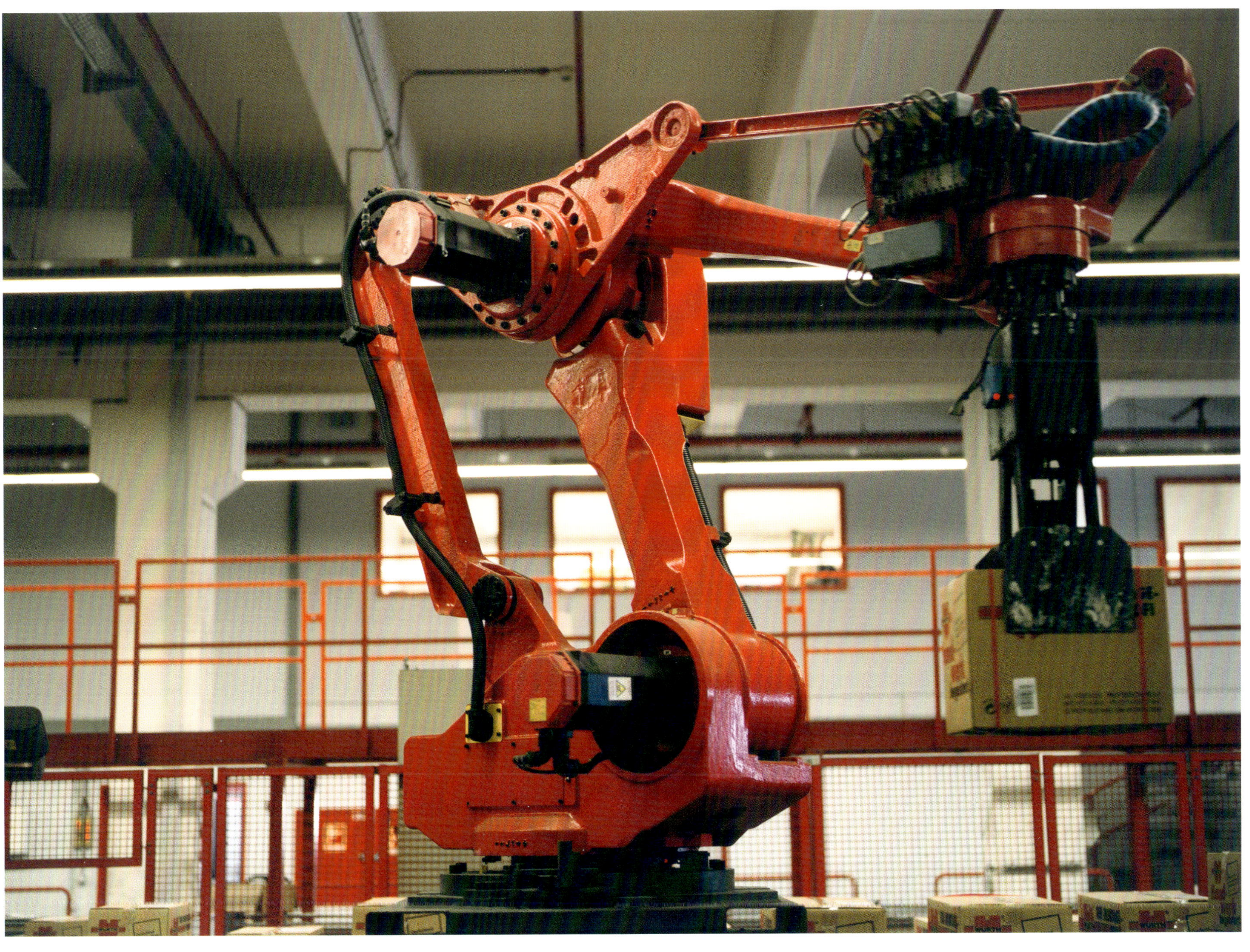

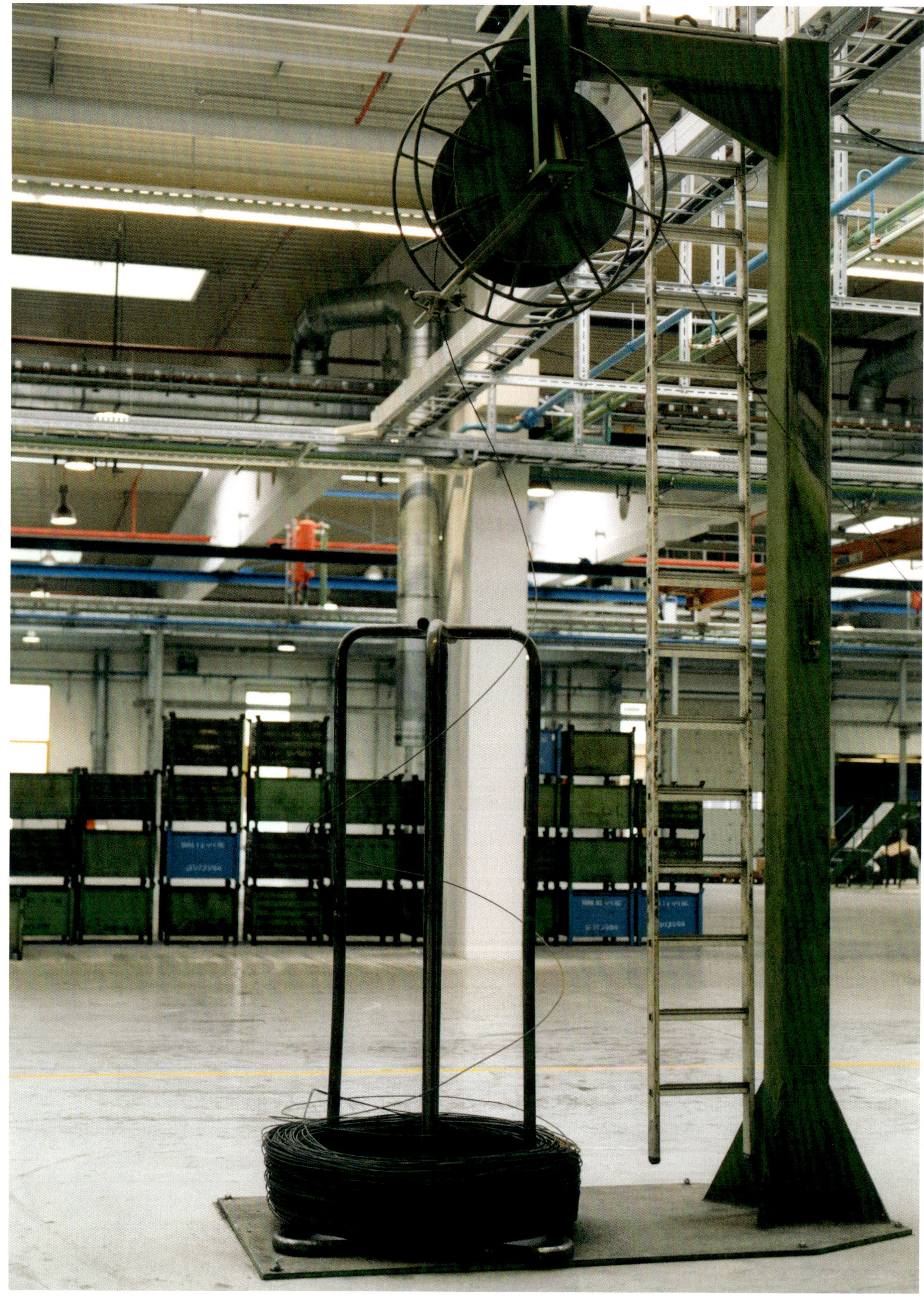

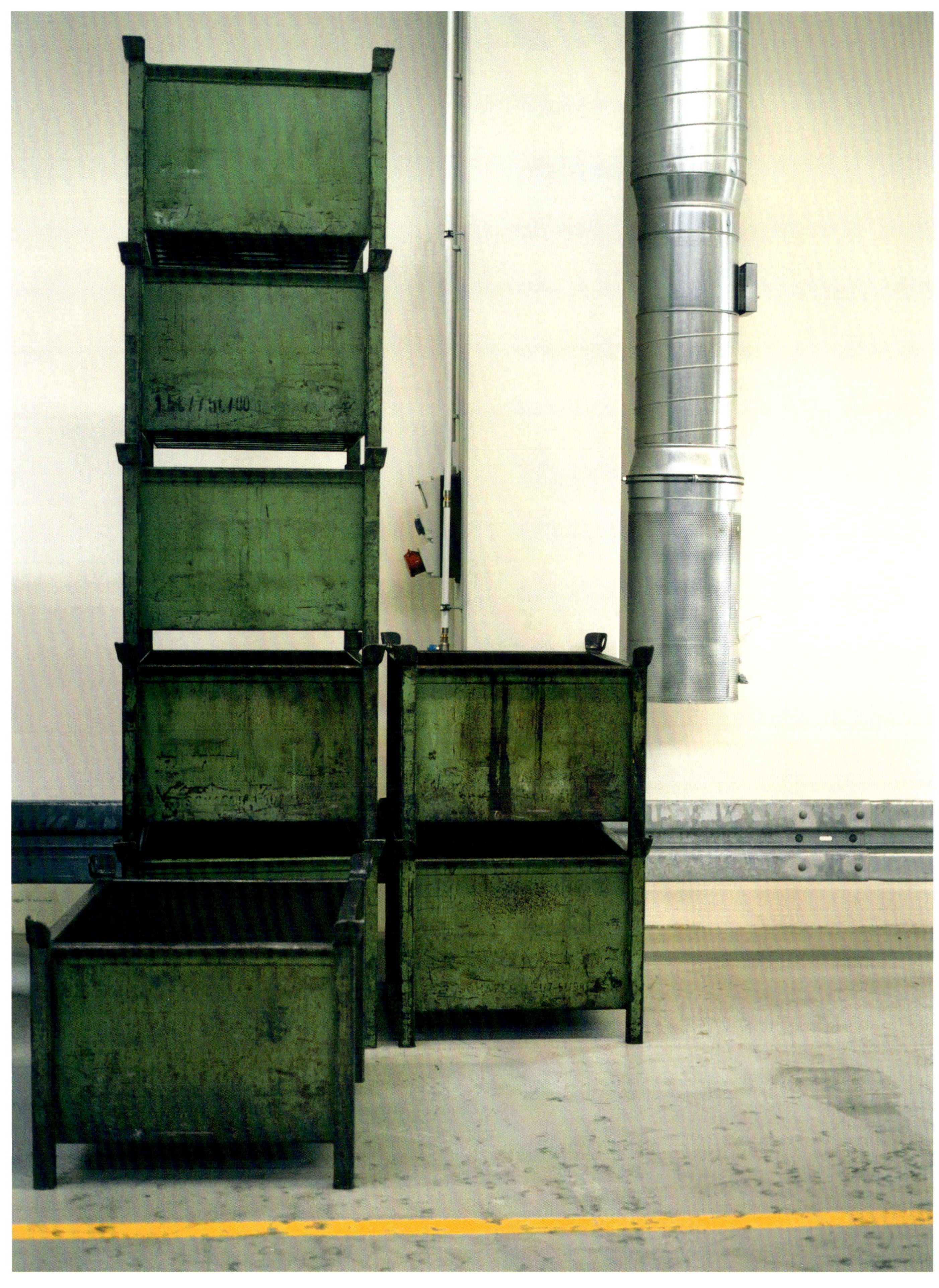

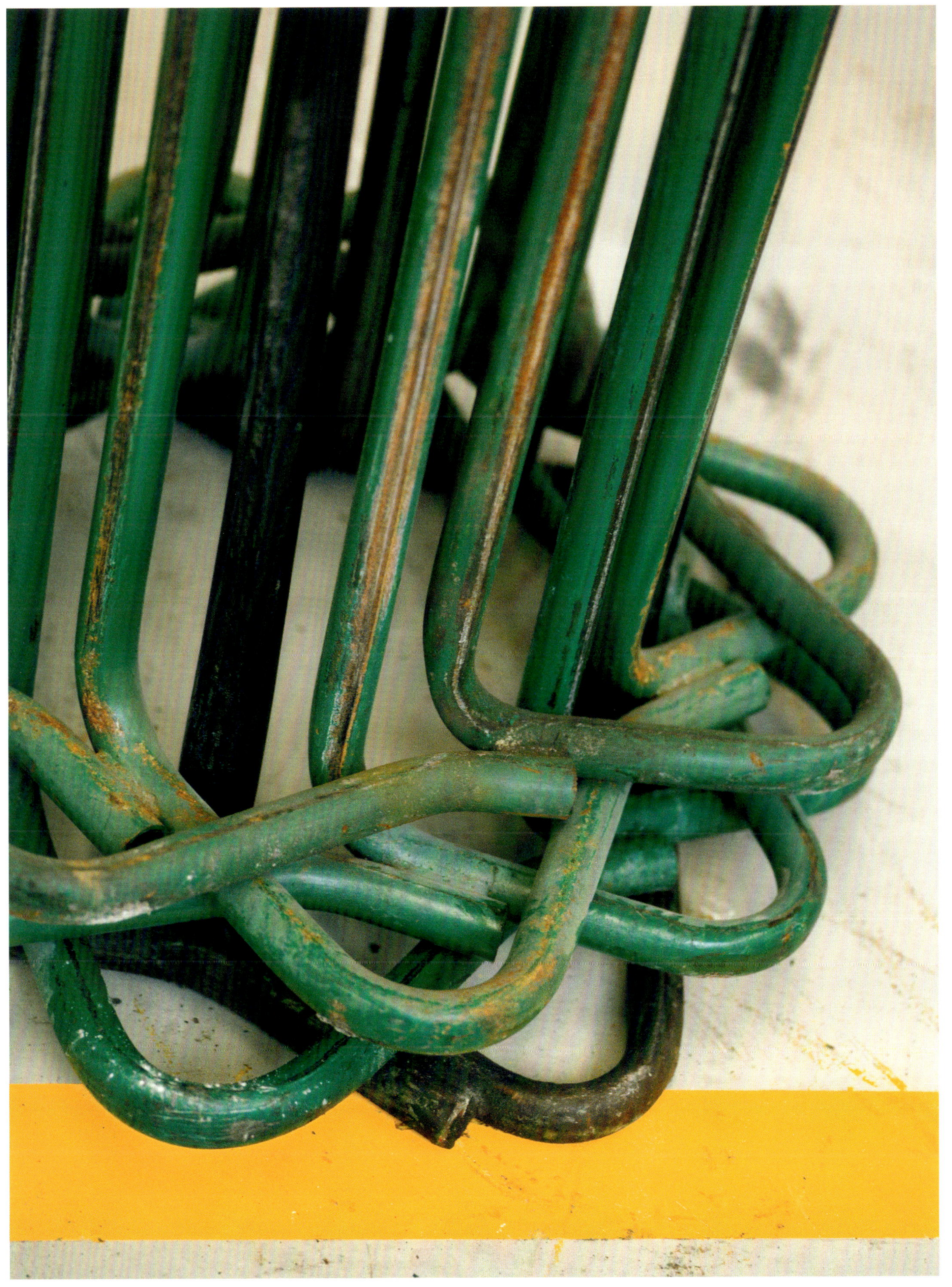

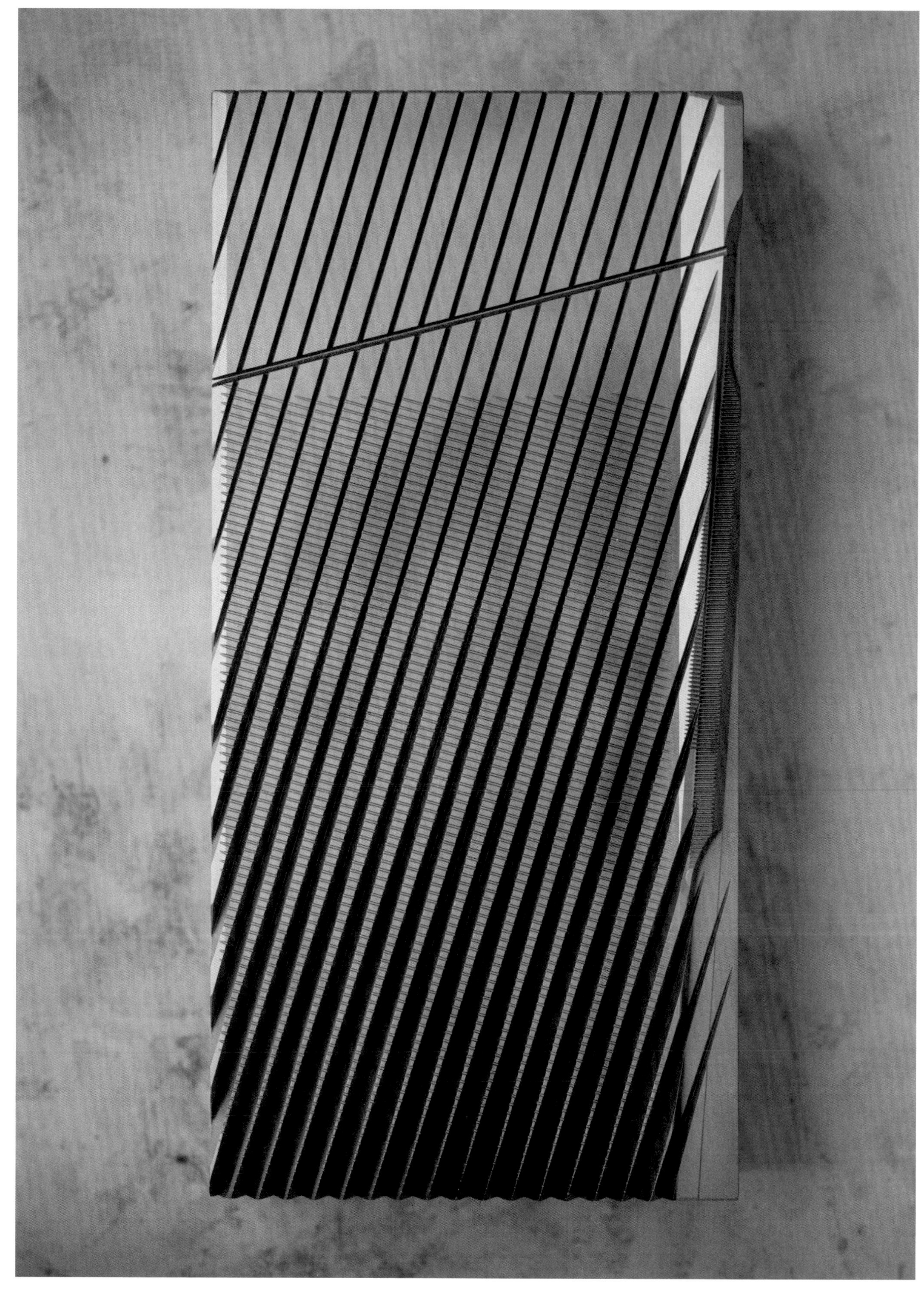

Bausch Decor GmbH
A SURTECO Company

Gründungsjahr Founded   2000
Dekorative Oberflächen Decorative Surfaces
Johan-Viktor-Bausch-Strasse 2
86647 Buttenwiesen

Eternit AG

Gründungsjahr Founded   1929
Faserzement Fiber cement
Im Breitspiel 20
69126 Heidelberg

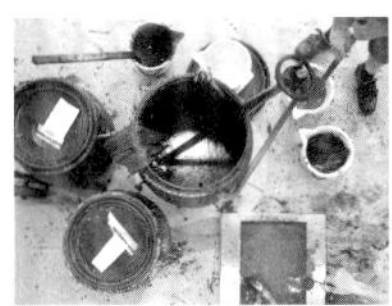

19 Rot Red
Bausch Decor, 2007

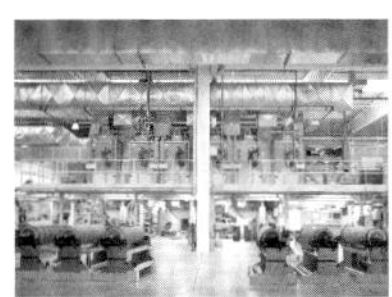

24 Halle Hall
Bausch Decor, 2007

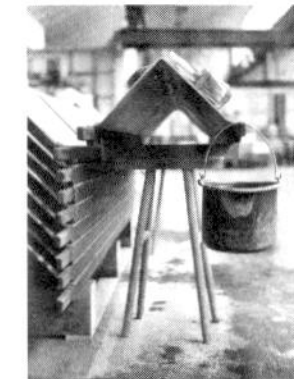

28 Manufactum Manufactum
Eternit, 2007

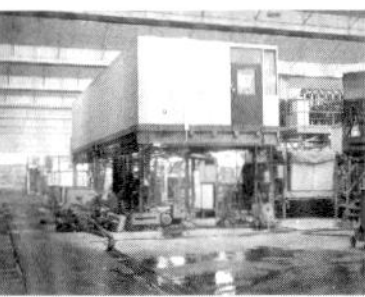

32–33 Halle Hall
Eternit, 2007

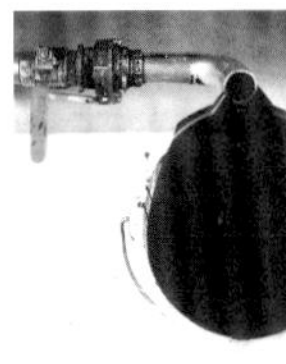

21 Eimer Bucket
Bausch Decor, 2007

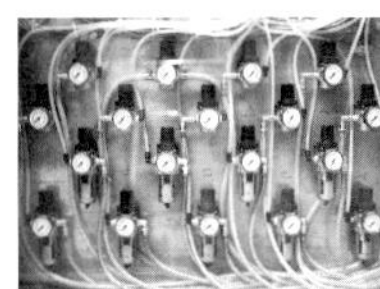

25 Druckluftssteuerung
Compressed air control
Bausch Decor, 2007

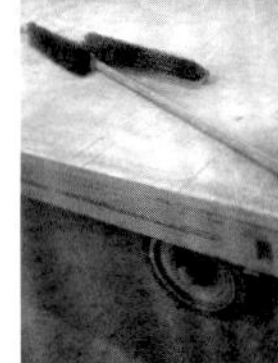

29 Besen Broom
Eternit, 2007

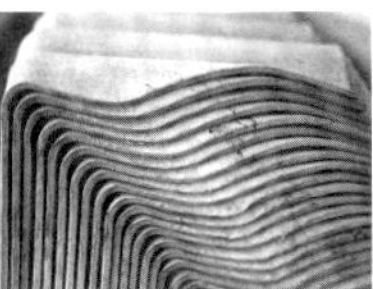

35 Wellpulthaube Corrugated capping
Eternit, 2007

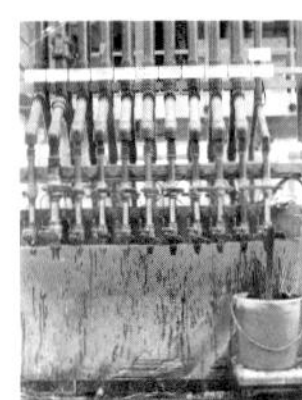

22 Farbentnahmestation
Color collection station
Bausch Decor, 2007

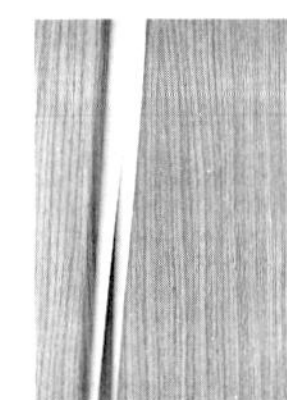

26 Maserung I Grain I
Bausch Decor, 2007

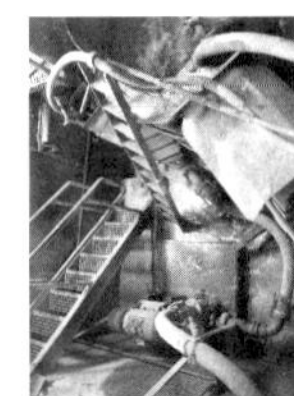

30 Wasser Water
Eternit, 2007

23 Farbabstrich Color scrape
Bausch Decor, 2007

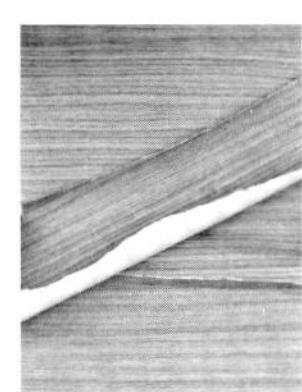

27 Maserung II Grain II
Bausch Decor, 2007

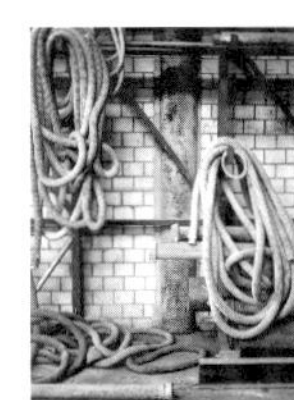

31 Schläuche Hoses
Eternit, 2007

Faber-Castell AG

Gründungsjahr Founded 1761
Schreibwaren Stationery
Nürnberger Strasse 2
90546 Stein

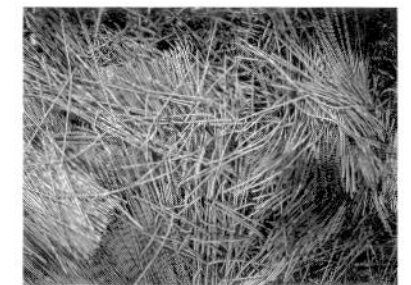

36 **Blei I** Lead I
Faber-Castell, 2006

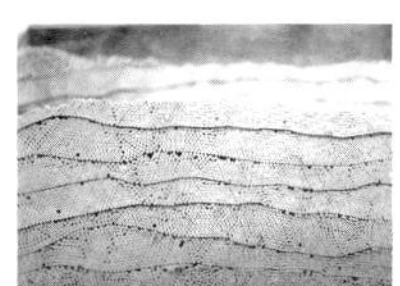

39 **Welle grün** Wave green
Faber-Castell, 2006

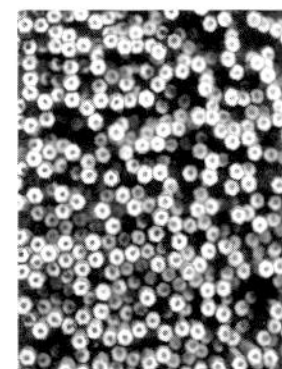

44 **Dots I** Dots I
Faber-Castell, 2006,

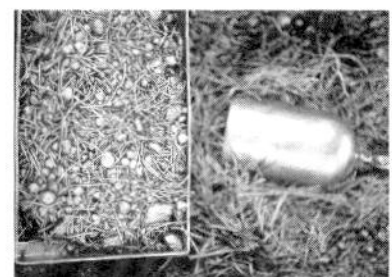

37 **Blei II** Lead II
Faber-Castell, 2006

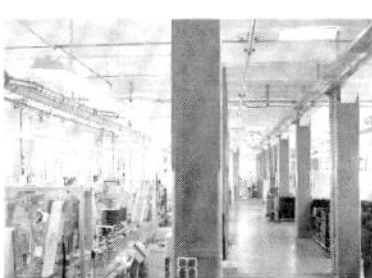

40–41 **Halle** Hall
Faber-Castell, 2006

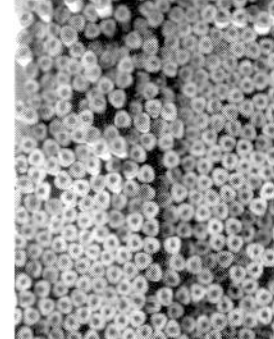

44 **Dots II** Dots II
Faber-Castell, 2006

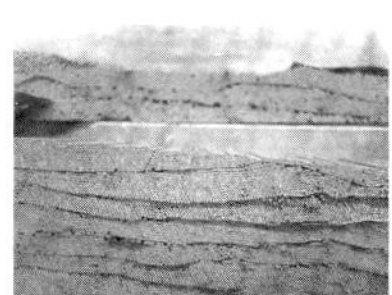

38 **Welle umbra** Wave umber
Faber-Castell, 2006

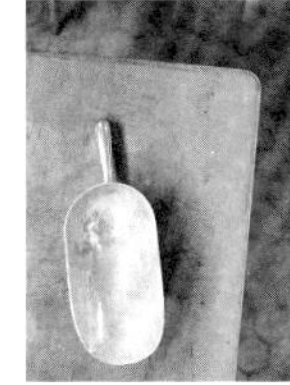

42 **Schaufel** Shovel
Faber-Castell, 2006

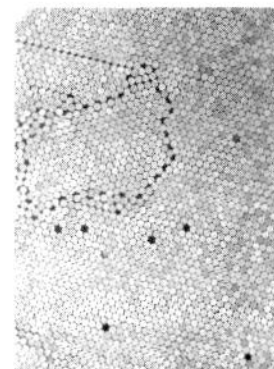

45 **Dots III** Dots III
Faber-Castell, 2006

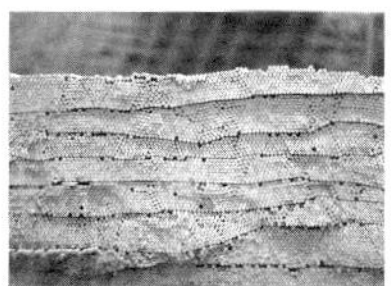

38 **Welle blau** Wave blue
Faber-Castell, 2006

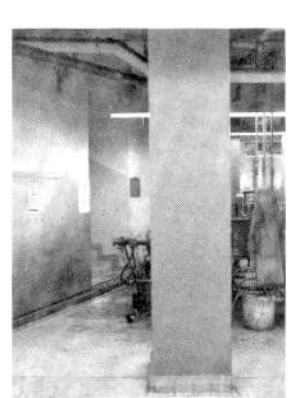

43 **Schürze** Apron
Faber-Castell, 2006

FALKE KGaA

Gründungsjahr Founded 1895
Bekleidung Apparel
Oststrasse 5
57392 Schmallenberg

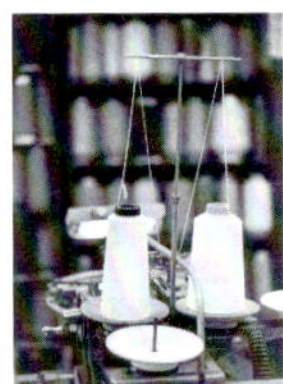

46 Garn Yarn
Falke, 2008

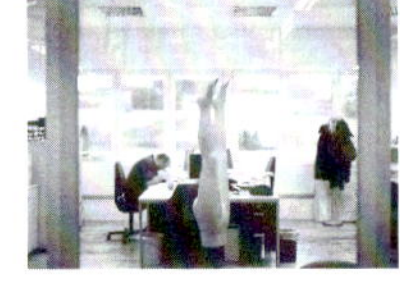

51 Beine Legs
Falke, 2008

47 Stuhl Chair
Falke, 2008

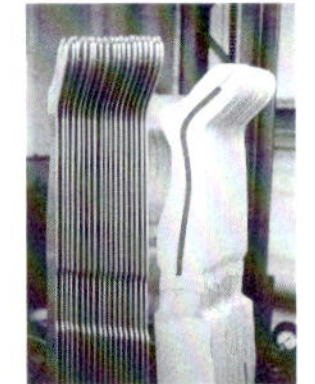

52 Strumpf Stocking
Falke, 2008

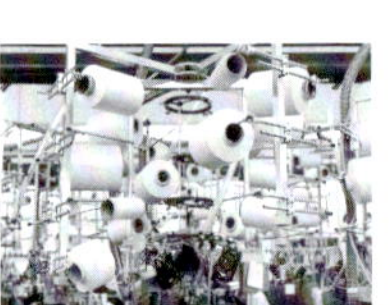

48–49 Nylon Nylon
Falke, 2008

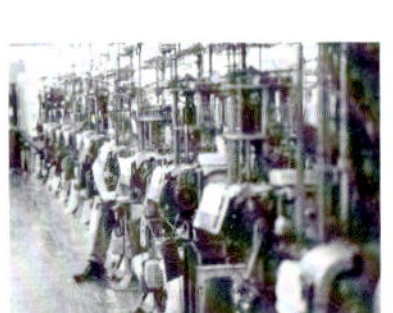

50 Fuß Foot
Falke, 2008

Giesecke & Devrient GmbH

Gründungsjahr Founded 1852
Banknoten- und Sicherheitspapier,
hergestellt in der Papierfabrik Louisenthal
Bank notes and safety paper, produced in
the Louisenthal paper factory
Prinzregentenstraße 159
81677 München

54 Baumwolle Cotton
Giesecke & Devrient, 2008

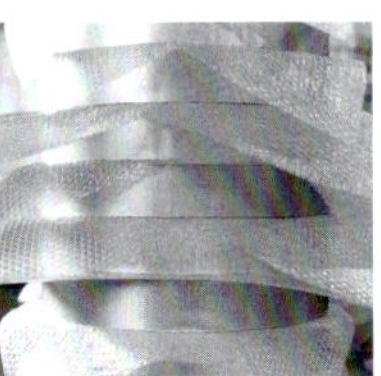

59 Sicherheitsfaden I
Safety thread I
Giesecke & Devrient, 2008

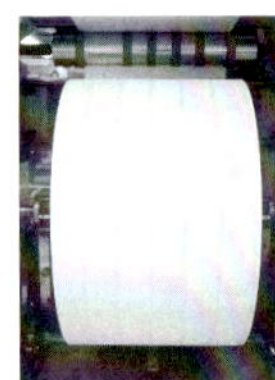

55 Effektfarben auf Banknotenpapier
Iridescent colors on banknote paper
Giesecke & Devrient, 2008

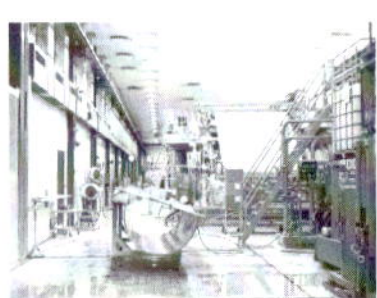

56–57 Halle Hall
Giesecke & Devrient, 2008

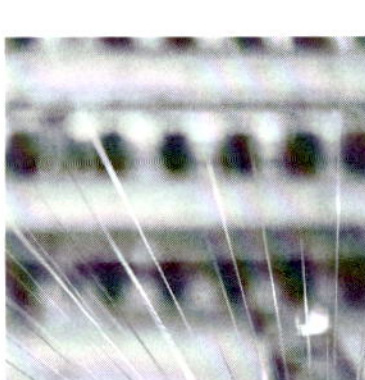

58 Sicherheitsfaden II
Safety thread II
Giesecke & Devrient, 2008

Dr. August Oetker Nahrungsmittel KG

Gründungsjahr Founded 1891
Nahrungsmittel Food
Lutterstrasse 14
33617 Bielefeld

Rectus AG

Gründungsjahr Founded 1950
Schnellverschlusskupplungen
Quick connect coupling systems
Daimlerstrasse 7
71735 Eberdingen

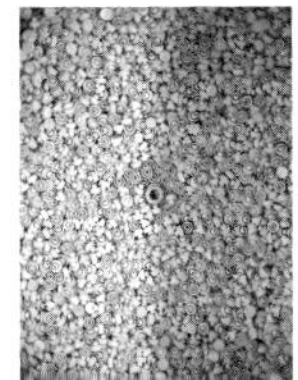

60   Aroma I   Flavor I
Dr. Oetker, 2008

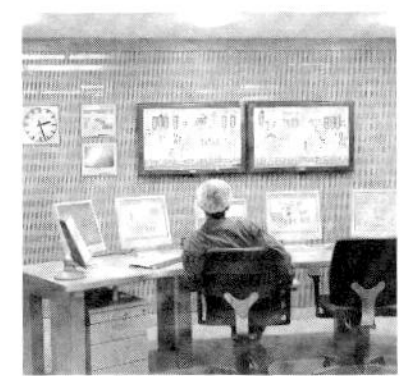

64   Zentrale   Control center
Dr. Oetker, 2008

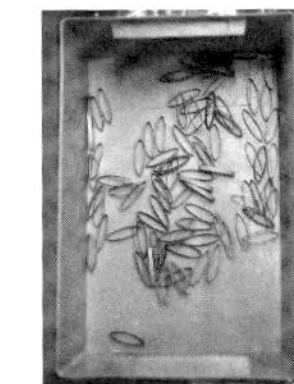

69   Blaue Kiste   Blue box
Rectus, 2007

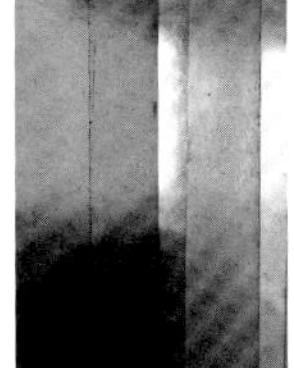

74   Vorhang I   Curtain I
Rectus, 2007

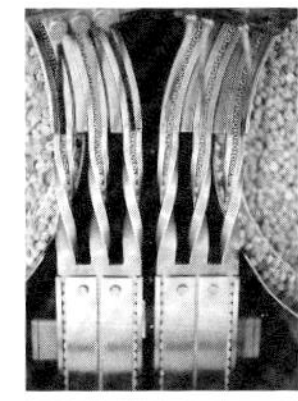

61   Aroma II   Flavor II
Dr. Oetker, 2008

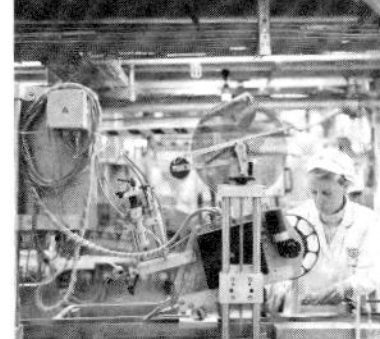

65   Dame   Lady
Dr. Oetker, 2008

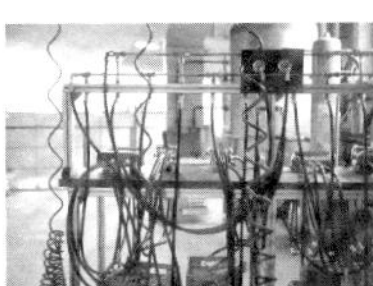

70   Schläuche   Hoses
Rectus, 2007

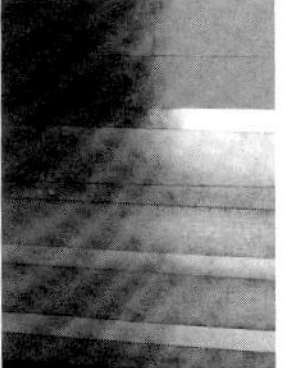

74   Vorhang II   Curtain II
Rectus, 2007

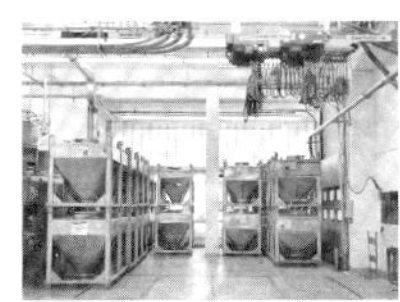

62   Mischung   Mixture
Dr. Oetker, 2008

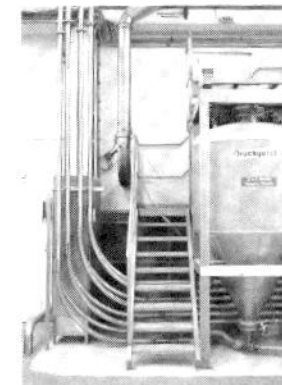

66   Druckgefäß   Pressure tank
Dr. Oetker, 2008

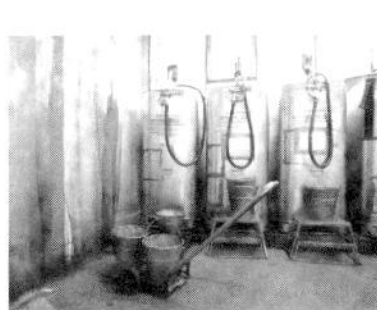

71   3000 Liter   3000 Liter
Rectus, 2007

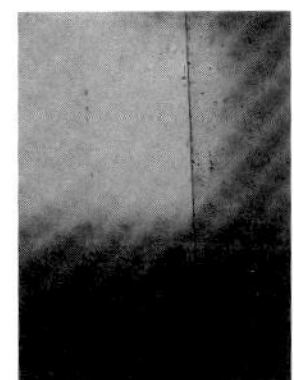

74   Vorhang III   Curtain III
Rectus, 2007

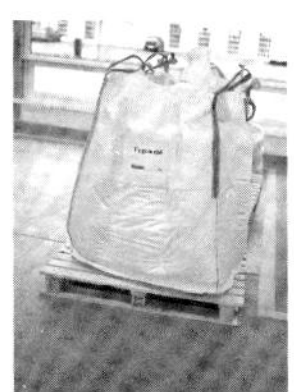

63   Fegemehl   Flour
Dr. Oetker, 2008

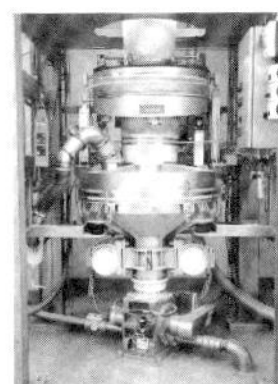

67   Nachschub   Supplies
Dr. Oetker, 2008

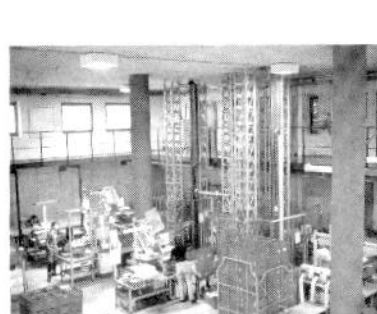

72–73   Halle   Hall
Rectus, 2007

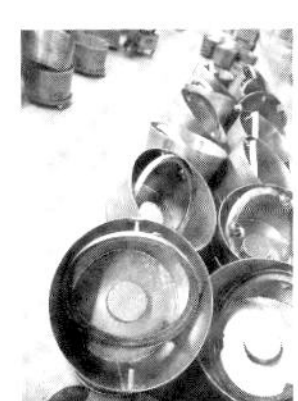

75   Spänekübel   Swarf tubs
Rectus, 2007

Schleich GmbH

Gründungsjahr Founded 1935
Spielwaren Toys
Am Limes 69
73527 Schwäbisch Gmünd

Villeroy & Boch AG

Gründungsjahr Founded 1748
Keramikhersteller Ceramics manufacturer
Saaruferstrasse
66693 Mettlach

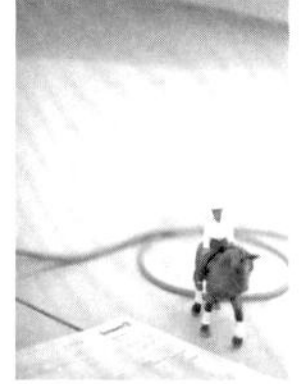

76 Cowboy Cowboy
Schleich, 2006

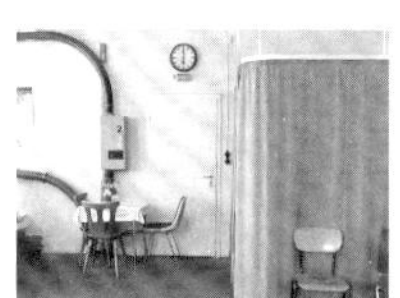

81 Pausenraum Break room
Schleich, 2006

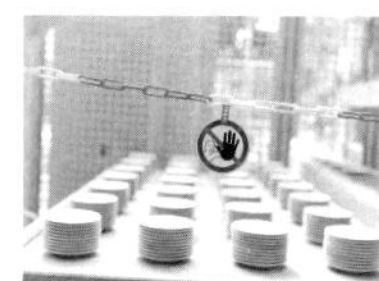

83 Stop Stop
Villeroy & Boch, 2006

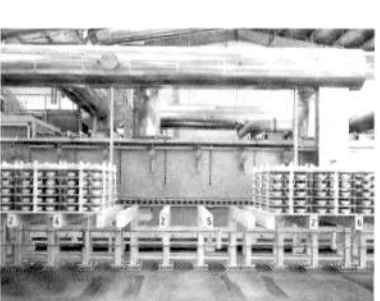

87 Zahlen Numbers
Villeroy & Boch, 2006

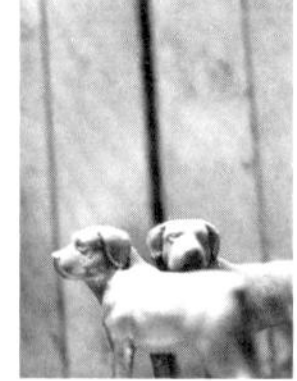

77 Hunde Dogs
Schleich, 2006

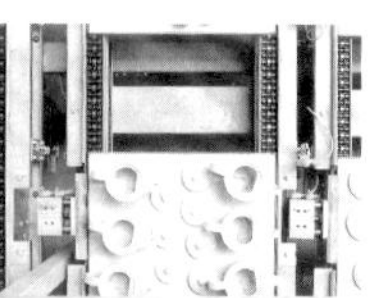

84 Kännchen Cannikins
Villeroy & Boch, 2006

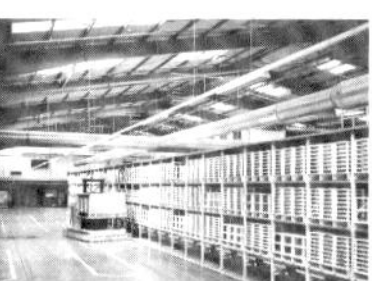

88 Halle Hall
Villeroy & Boch, 2006

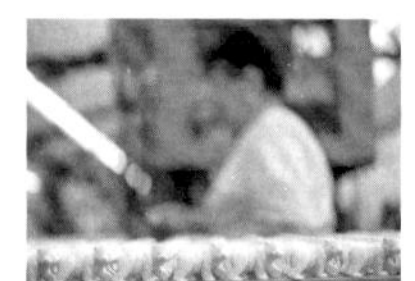

78–79 Knut Knut
Schleich, 2006

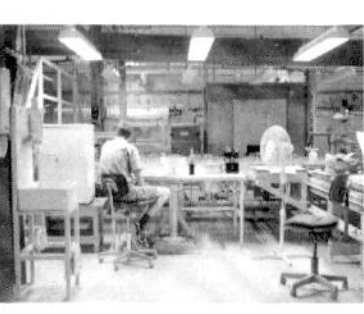

85 Waschbecken Washbasin
Villeroy & Boch, 2006

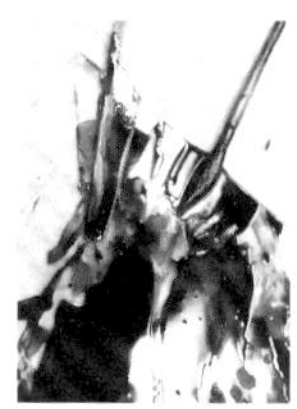

89 Gold Gold
Villeroy & Boch, 2006

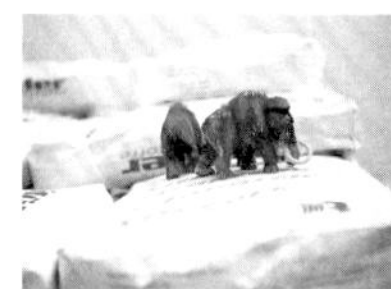

80 Ice Age Ice Age
Schleich, 2006

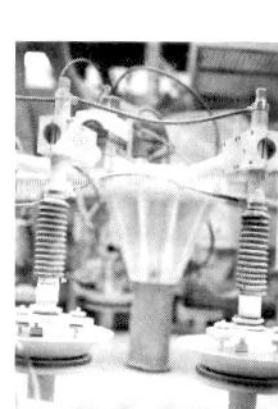

86 Teller Plate
Villeroy & Boch, 2006

Würth-Gruppe

Gründungsjahr Founded 1945
Adolf Würth GmbH & Co. KG
Schraubengroßhandlung und -herstellung
Distribution and production of screws
Reinhold-Würth-Strasse
74653 Künzelsau

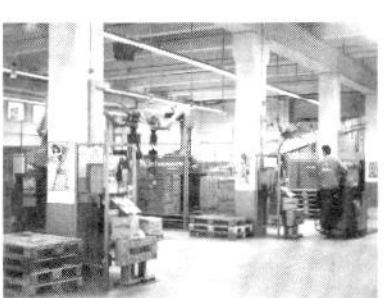

90 Pin up Pin up
Würth, 2007

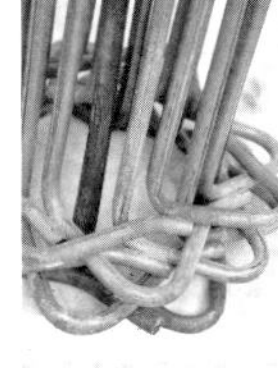

95 Kronenständer Crown stands
Würth, 2007

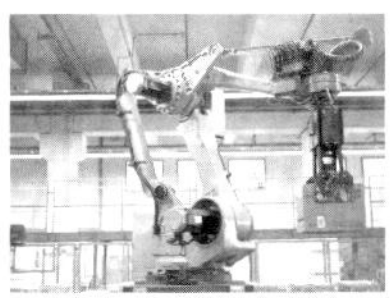

91 Roboter Robot
Würth, 2007

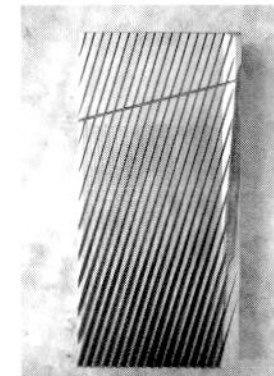

96 Walzbacke Thread rolling dias
Würth, 2007

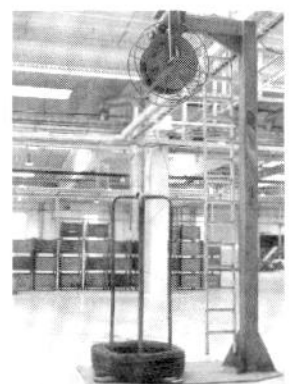

92 Drahtvorziehgerät
Wire drawing
Würth, 2007

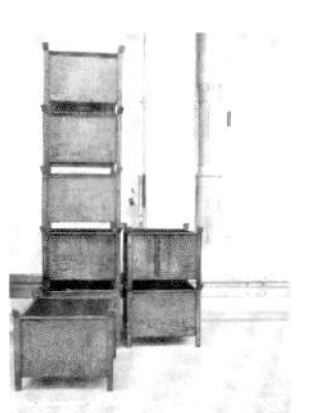

94 Kisten Boxes
Würth, 2007

PHILINE VON SELL

Philine von Sell wurde 1963 in Hamburg geboren.

In den Achtzigerjahren gründete sie als Regisseurin eine Produktionsfirma für Werbefilme und arbeitete für Werbeagenturen und Unternehmen. Philine von Sell wurde 1996 an die Hochschule für Fernsehen und Film München berufen und baute dort den Lehrstuhl für Werbe-, PR- und Imagefilm auf. 1998 ging Philine von Sell nach Südafrika. Sie begann dort als Fotografin zu arbeiten, gründete im Jahr 2000 die Hilforganisation LifeTime e. V. zur Unterstützung von Aidswaisen und initiierte ein Projekt zur Begabtenförderung in den Townships. 2004 kehrte sie nach Deutschland zurück und realisiert seitdem, gemeinsam mit ihrem Mann Philipp von Sell, Film- und Kunstprojekte.

Philine von Sell lebt und arbeitet in Berlin.

EINZELAUSSTELLUNGEN

1998
Steine I. Phase. Lesbare Gesichter, Europa-Center, Berlin
1999/2000
LifeTime. The Children of Nazareth House,[1] Castle of Good Hope, Kapstadt; Kantdreieck, Berlin; Art Cologne, Köln; Madibas Village, Johannesburg
2004/05
Growing Creativity. The LifeTime Gallery Project,[2] Museum Africa, Johannesburg; Art Forum Berlin; Gesseau Art Gallery, Johannesburg
2006
Made in Germany Phase I, Projektgalerie HofmannVonSell, Berlin
2007
LifeTime. The Children of Nazareth House, Projektgalerie HofmannVonSell, Berlin
2008
Made in Germany Phase II, Konrad-Adenauer-Stiftung, Berlin

AUSZEICHNUNGEN

Als Autorin und Regisseurin erhielt Philine von Sell von 1989 bis 2002 für ihre Filme 24 nationale und internationale Auszeichnungen.

ÖFFENTLICHE SAMMLUNG

Kunstsammlung des Deutschen Bundestages

1 Über das Leben aidskranker Kinder. Aus den intensiven Begegnungen und Erlebnissen entstanden Fotografien, Film- und Tonaufnahmen (Kapstadt).
2 Für dieses Projekt inspirierte Philine von Sell junge Leute in den Townships, kreativ tätig zu werden. Sie führte sie in Künstlerzirkeln zusammen und ermöglichte ihnen ein freies und künstlerisches Arbeiten (Gauteng, Western Cape und Venda).

PHILINE VON SELL

Philine von Sell was born in Hamburg in 1963.

During the nineteen-eighties she founded a production company for advertisements and worked for several advertising agencies. In 1996, she was appointed to the University of Television and Film in Munich and established the department for advertising and promotional film. In 1998 she went to South Africa, where she began working as a photographer and where she founded the organization LifeTime, a project that supports children orphaned by AIDS. In addition, von Sell initiated an education program for gifted youth in the townships. Since von Sell returned to Germany in 2004, she has been working on film and art projects with her husband, Philipp von Sell.

Philine von Sell lives and works in Berlin.

INDIVIDUAL EXHIBITIONS

1998
Steine I. Phase. Lesbare Gesichter, Europa-Center, Berlin
1999/2000
LifeTime. The Children of Nazareth House,[1] Castle of Good Hope, Kapstadt; Kantdreieck, Berlin; Art Cologne, Köln; Madibas Village, Johannesburg
2004/05
Growing Creativity. The LifeTime Gallery Project,[2] Museum Africa, Johannesburg; Art Forum Berlin; Gesseau Art Gallery, Johannesburg
2006
Made in Germany Phase I, Projektgalerie HofmannVonSell, Berlin
2007
LifeTime. The Children of Nazareth House, Projektgalerie HofmannVonSell, Berlin
2008
Made in Germany Phase II, Konrad-Adenauer-Stiftung, Berlin

AWARDS

As an author and director, Philine von Sell received 24 national and international awards for her films between 1989 and 2002.

PUBLIC COLLECTION

Art Collection of the German Parliament

1   The Lives of Children with AIDS. Von Sell's poignant encounters and experiences resulted in photographs, film, and audio material (Capetown).
2   For this project, Philine von Sell inspired young people in the townships to work creatively. She brought them together into artists' circles, enabled them to work freely and creatively (Gauteng, Western Cape, and Venda).

DANK

Ich möchte mich bei allen bedanken, die mich von Beginn an bei
Made in Germany begleitet und unterstützt haben. Besonderer Dank
gilt Hans-Jörg Clement und Peter W. Klein, des Weiteren dem
Fine-Art-Printer Erwin Rittenschober und Joseph Gallus Rittenberg.

Den beteiligten Unternehmen danke ich für ihr Vertrauen, mir
Zutritt in ihre Produktionsstätten zu gewähren.

ACKNOWLEGDMENTS

I would like to thank all those who have accompanied and supported
me from the outset of this project. I am especially grateful to
Hans-Jörg Clement and Peter W. Klein, and also to the fine art printer
Erwin Rittenschober and to Joseph Gallus Rittenberg.

I am also indebted to the companies for their trust and for
granting me access to their production sites.

Herausgeber   Editor   Hans-Jörg Clement
Verlagslektorat   Copyediting   Donna Stonecipher, Clemens von Lucius
Übersetzungen   Translations   Benjamin Letzler
Grafische Gestaltung   Graphic design   Antonia Neubacher, Berlin
Schrift   Typeface   DIN Alternate
Reproduktionen   Reproductions   hausstætter herstellung, Berlin
Papier   Paper   Galaxi Supermat, 200 g/m²
Druck   Printing   sellier druck GmbH, Freising
Buchbinderei   Binding   Conzella Verlagsbuchbinderei, Urban Meister GmbH,
Aschheim-Dornach bei München

Erschienen im   Published by   Hatje Cantz Verlag
Zeppelinstrasse 32, 73760 Ostfildern, Deutschland   Germany
Tel. +49 711 4405-200, Fax +49 711 4405-220
www.hatjecantz.com

Hatje Cantz books are available internationally at selected bookstores.
For more information about our distribution partners please visit our homepage at www.hatjecantz.com.

ISBN 978-3-7757-2198-1

Printed in Germany

Umschlagabbildungen   Cover illustrations
Vorne   Front cover   Druckbehälter   Pressure tank   Rectus, 2007
Hinten   Back cover   Schaufel   Shovel   Faber-Castell, 2006